# Dan Beard

## Scoutmaster of America

# Dan Beard

## SCOUTMASTER OF AMERICA

by Wyatt Blassingame

illustrated by Dom Lupo

GARRARD PUBLISHING COMPANY
CHAMPAIGN, ILLINOIS

# Contents

# 1

# The River

The bank of the Ohio River was steep and muddy. Four boys stood at the top, looking down. "If we poured a little more water down this bank," Dan Beard said, "it would make a fine slide."

"The mud would ruin our pants," his cousin Bob said.

"Not if we take them off," Dan said. "There's nobody around to see us."

Quickly the four boys took off their clothes and went down to the river. They found an old bucket with a hole in the bottom. They carried water to the top of the bank and poured it down. Soon the bank was wet and slippery.

"Watch!" Dan shouted. With a running start he slid down the bank. He shot off the bottom and hit the water with a great splash. After him came the other boys. By the time the last one was in the water, Dan was sliding down the bank again. Each time a boy went down the bank, the slide got wetter and faster.

"Look!" Bob called.

Standing in the water, Dan turned and looked upstream. Around the bend in the river came a raft made of big logs fastened together. In the middle of the raft was a small cabin. Tied to one corner of the cabin was a cow. Nearby, a woman washed clothes in a large pot. At the end of the raft stood a man holding a long oar. By pushing this to one side or the other, he could make the raft drift right or left. A small boy sat near him, fishing.

From the water Dan and his friends watched the raft drift past. They waved to the boy who was fishing, and he waved back.

"That's the third raft I've seen this week," Bob said. "Where do you think they're going?"

"Missouri maybe," Ed Hunter replied. "When they find some good land along the river, they just stop. Then they build a cabin and start farming. That's what my father says they do."

"Maybe they're going all the way out West," Dan said. He watched the raft as it drifted out of sight. "There are still buffalo out there," Dan said. "And Indians. I wish I was going with those people."

"Where we'd better go," Bob said, "is home. It's getting late."

The boys climbed out of the river and put on their clothes. Then they started for home in the small city of Cincinnati, Ohio.

Dan's home was on John Street, which ran down to the river. As the boys neared Dan's house, they heard loud squealing and grunting noises behind them.

The boys turned to see that the street was filled with pigs. After the pigs came

three men with long sticks, driving the pigs ahead of them.

"Come on," Dan shouted. "Let's play Indians and buffalo! The pigs are the buffalo!"

The boys waited until all the pigs had passed; then they joined the men driving them. Whooping and shouting, they "galloped" back and forth behind the pigs.

They pretended to shoot them with bows and arrows. The pigs squealed and ran.

"You boys make good pig drivers," one of the men said, laughing.

By the time Dan got home, it was dark. His family was already eating supper. Dan had three older brothers and two little sisters.

Dan's mother took one look at him. "Go wash your face and hands now," she ordered. "Your clothes are a mess. Where have you been?"

Dan's brother Frank began to laugh. "I can tell you where Danny's been. He's been swimming, or walking in the woods, or maybe trying to tame a wild rabbit. Anyway, he's been out in the country. That's where Danny always is when he has a chance."

# 2

# "I'll Knock You Off That Wagon!"

Dan's father was a well-known artist. Famous people often visited him to have their pictures painted. One day Dan met a man named Rutherford B. Hayes in his father's studio. Later he met another one named James Garfield. Both of these men would become presidents of the United States. Now they were just grown-ups in whom Dan had little interest.

Dan was far more interested in the pictures of rivers, trees, and wild animals that his father sometimes painted.

Dan liked to watch his father paint. Sometimes Dan would draw pictures himself. Since he usually had a houseful of pets, he used them for models. He drew pictures of his pet raccoon, his pet crow, and even his pet snakes. Drawing seemed easy and natural for him. He began to draw so well that the drawing teacher at school sometimes let him teach the class.

One day the teacher said, "I must go to the principal's office for a few minutes. While I'm gone, I want Dan to show the class how to draw a picture of a house."

Proud of himself, Dan went to the blackboard. He drew a picture of a house with trees around it and a dog in the yard. Then he began to grin. Quickly he drew a funny picture of the drawing teacher wearing her big hooped skirt. Behind him, some of the students began to giggle.

Beside the teacher, Dan drew a picture of the principal. It showed him spanking one of the students with a big board.

Now all of the boys and girls were laughing. They were making so much noise that they didn't hear the teacher coming down the hall. Suddenly Dan heard her and quickly erased all the pictures except the house.

The angry teacher entered the room. "You should be sorry!" she told them. "Dan has been trying to teach you to draw. Instead of learning, you're all laughing at him!"

No one in the class told why they had really been laughing. Dan felt sorry the class had been blamed for his joke. But he wasn't sorry enough to tell on himself.

On his way home from school, Dan often walked along the river. He would see riverboats with big paddle wheels tied to the docks. Men sang as they loaded and unloaded cargo and animals. Pigs and cattle squealed and bellowed.

It was the river itself that attracted Dan the most. He watched longingly as the flatboats and rafts moved downstream. Both his father and grandfather had told him stories of the wilderness to the west. The forests along the Ohio and the

Mississippi rivers had once been filled with wild game. Now those forests were disappearing. Beyond the rivers lay the great plains, and beyond the plains were high wild mountains. Many people were now moving westward beyond the rivers. More and more of these wagon trains carrying settlers traveled slowly toward California and Oregon. Often there were battles with Indians who feared that the settlers would take their land.

What would the West be like when he grew up? Dan wondered.

One day Dan was walking home when he saw a wagon stuck in the mud beside the river. The driver was a big, ugly man. He shouted at his horses and beat them with his whip. The horses tried hard to pull the wagon out of the mud. But they could not work together because of the beating. The driver became more angry

and kept beating the horses. The wagon sank deeper in the mud.

Dan stood and watched. He became so angry that he forgot he was only a boy. "Stop beating those horses!" he shouted. "Stop it!"

The driver turned his head and looked at Dan. "Aw shut up," he said. Once more he began to beat the horses.

"Stop it!" Dan shouted. He picked up a large rock. "If you don't stop, I'll knock you off that wagon!"

This time the driver turned and stared at the small boy. "Why, you little brat," he said. "I'll—"

What might have happened, Dan never knew. A group of blue-coated soldiers had been standing nearby. Now they moved forward. "The boy's right," one of them told the driver. "It won't help to beat the horses. We'll help you."

Speaking kindly to the horses, the soldiers got the wagon moving and out of the mud.

In the days that followed, Dan saw more and more soldiers. At home he heard talk about a possible war between the North and the South.

In the South some people owned slaves. Dan's family and most people in the North thought slavery was wrong. There seemed to be no way to settle the question peacefully.

One day Dan's father came running into the house. "Caroline," he told his wife, "the South has fired on Fort Sumter! The war has begun!"

It was April 1861, just two months before Daniel Carter Beard's eleventh birthday.

# 3

# The First Boone Scouts

Soon after the start of the Civil War, the Beard family moved to Covington, Kentucky. This was a small town just across the Ohio River from Cincinnati. Here Dan's father joined the Northern army. Soon all three of his older brothers went to war too. Only eleven-year-old Dan was left with his mother and his two little sisters. Now he was the man of the family.

Dan liked living in Covington. Nearby, the Licking River flowed into the Ohio. Just a few miles away was a third stream called Bank Lick. This was a very tiny, clear creek that wound its way through a small forest.

Dan's four best friends in Covington were named Jim, Tom, Harry, and Dick. In the summer the five boys often walked the dusty road that led from the town to Bank Lick. The boys carried their lunches in paper bags. They spent the day fishing, swimming, and playing games.

One day Dan noticed a long grapevine that hung from a tree over the middle of the creek. "Hey," he said. "I've got an idea."

"You're always getting ideas," Harry said.

Dan reached for the grapevine with a long stick and pulled it to the bank.

Carefully he tested the vine to see if it would hold his weight. "Now watch," he said. He grabbed the vine firmly. Then taking a running start, he swung all the way across the creek and dropped on the far bank.

One by one the other boys followed.

"We could make a fine hideout over here," Jim exclaimed. "Nobody would ever find us!"

"All right," Dan said. "We could be scouts like Daniel Boone. We could call ourselves the Boone Scouts."

From this time on, Dan and his friends were the Boone Scouts. Their hideout was a cave they dug in a bank near the creek. The opening was hidden by thick bushes. Here, day after day, they played that they were frontier scouts and Indians. They pretended to hunt deer and buffalo. Sometimes they camped out over the weekend. They cooked food over open fires and slept on beds made of pine needles.

"My grandfather says there used to be buffalo, right here in Kentucky," Dan said one day.

"Well, they're not here anymore," Tom said. "I never saw a buffalo in my life."

"Where did they go?" Dick asked.

The boys were sitting around a campfire

in front of their hideout. They looked at one another, but nobody answered. "Grandfather says there used to be a million wild parakeets in these woods," Dan said. "There were passenger pigeons too. Grandfather says that they traveled south in the winter. Sometimes there were so many passenger pigeons flying over he couldn't see the sky."

"I've seen passenger pigeons and wild parakeets," Tom said. "Lots of them."

"But not a million at a time," Dan said.

"People used to shoot so many of the passenger pigeons they couldn't eat them all," Harry said. "They'd just throw them away."

"Do you think the passenger pigeons and the wild parakeets will ever disappear like the buffalo?" Dan asked.

"Of course not," Tom said. "There are too many of them." He stood up. "I'm

hungry. Dan, show us how to cook those eggs you brought."

"All right," Dan said. "We need some mud from the creek."

All the boys got handfuls of mud. Dan molded the mud around each egg until it was the size of a baseball. Then he put the balls in hot ashes close to the fire. "Daniel Boone used to cook wild turkey eggs this way," he said. "Lots of frontier scouts did."

"Soldiers sometimes cook eggs this way too," Jim said.

"That's right," Dan said. "I'll bet that Morgan's raiders cook eggs like this."

The boys began to talk about General John Morgan, a famous cavalry officer in the Southern army. For the past few months General Morgan's soldiers had been making raids behind the Northern lines in Kentucky and in Tennessee. "Do you think his raiders might come here?" Harry asked.

"Naw," Tom said.

"I'll bet they could," Harry said. "They ride along the back roads and through the woods, and—"

Suddenly there was a sharp *bang!* Then another and another. Ashes flew up from the campfire. "The raiders!" Harry yelled. "They're shooting at us!"

The boys jumped to their feet. They started to run, falling over one another. Then they all turned and dived back into their cave.

There was another loud bang. All at once Dan started to laugh. "Nobody's shooting at us," he said.

"Then what—?"

"It's the eggs," Dan said. "I forgot to make a small hole in each egg so the air could get out. That's why they blew up."

# 4
# The War

The Boone Scouts stood close beside the fence in Dan's yard. Wide-eyed, they watched soldiers march past at double time. An officer on a black horse raced by in the other direction. Big guns drawn by mules rumbled past.

"The whole Northern army must be here," Dan said. "I wonder why?"

"I know," Harry said. "The newspaper says that old General Kirby Smith has a

Southern army on the other side of Bank Lick. There's going to be a battle."

"When?"

"I don't know. Today maybe."

"Come on," Dan said. "Let's go watch."

"We might get shot," Harry and Jim said together.

"Not if we're careful."

Keeping close together, the boys went down the sidewalk. There were soldiers everywhere. At the head of Garrard Street, a whole regiment was camped.

Outside the town the boys saw even more soldiers all over the hillsides. A few days before, these same hills had been covered with wild flowers. Now all the flowers were beaten into the ground. A small brook flowing between the hills was filthy with mud, old papers, and bottles.

"They sure make a mess," Dan said. "I wonder what's happened to our hideout."

"I'll bet the Southern soldiers are using it for a camp," Tom said.

"Naw," Jim said. "They are way south of Bank Lick. At least that's what I heard."

"Let's go find out."

The other boys stared at Dan. "You mean—?"

"We'll be the Boone Scouts," Dan said. "We'll move along quietly through the trees. If we see any enemy soldiers, we can go back and tell our soldiers where they are."

The boys looked around them carefully and talked in whispers. They started along a path they knew. But now it was hard to find and looked dangerous. They had gone almost a mile when far off to the right they heard the sound of a rifle. Then came another shot, and another. After that it was quiet.

"I think we'd better go back," Harry said.

"We're almost there," Dan said. "Come on."

Moving carefully from tree to tree, the boys reached Bank Lick. They crossed on their grapevine swing. The hideout was safe; no one had been there. The boys were happy that their camping ground was safe.

Going home, the boys reached the edge of the woods without seeing any soldiers. Before turning onto the path, they could see ahead a hillside dotted here and there with trees. Suddenly one of the trees split wide open. Its top came crashing down. Moments later they heard the sound of a cannon, far away. The cannonball had hit the tree.

"Who—who do you think they are shooting at?" Harry asked.

"I don't know," Dan said. "But we'd better get away from here." They ran along the path, back to the road, and all the way into Covington.

The boys never did learn where the cannonball came from or why it was fired. No battle during the war was fought close to Covington. General Kirby Smith and his soldiers retreated South. Not long afterward most of the Northern soldiers left Covington also.

Elsewhere, however, the war went on. Then one April night in 1865, Dan awoke to what sounded like gunfire close by. He jumped out of bed and ran downstairs. His mother and sisters were already on the porch. Across the river they could see rockets flashing through the dark sky. "Southern troops must have captured Cincinnati," Dan's mother said.

Soon they heard men shouting, louder

and still louder. "Richmond has fallen! Hooray! Northern soldiers have captured Richmond!"

Mrs. Beard put her arms around her three children. "Thank God," she said. "Our soldiers have captured Richmond, the Southern capital. This means the war is almost over. Your father and brothers will soon be home safe."

# 5

# Adventures As a Surveyor

"Danny," Mr. Beard said, "what kind of work do you want to do for a living?"

The Civil War was over now, and Mr. Beard was back home.

"Well," Dan said, "I could be an artist like you."

Mr. Beard smiled. "It's a very uncertain way of earning a living. An artist can't always sell his paintings. There must be something else you want to do."

"What I really want," Dan said, "is a job that will keep me out of doors."

"How about engineering?" Mr. Beard asked. "You're good at figures."

The idea pleased Dan. For the next few years, he went to school at Worrall's Academy. At nineteen he graduated and set out to find a job.

The only engineering job that Dan could find was one that paid him exactly nothing. But it did give him experience. He worked hard; he kept studying. Before long he was offered a good job as a surveyor with a map and publishing company.

Dan's new job kept him out of doors. It also gave him a chance to travel. He moved from town to town drawing maps of the streets and houses. Sometimes, to get a better view, Dan climbed up to the roof of the highest building.

In Wheeling, West Virginia, he went to the roof of a tall factory building. He still could not see what he wanted. At the edge of the building's roof was a brick chimney six feet high. Carefully Dan climbed to the top of it. He stood up and began to make his drawing.

Suddenly one of the bricks under Dan's foot gave way. He tried to regain his balance, waving his arms wildly. If he fell forward, he would fall many feet. He managed to fall backward, off the chimney and onto the roof. His leg doubled under him.

At first Dan thought that his leg was broken, but it was not. For many years though, his knee would suddenly go out of place. To straighten it, he would have to squat down wherever he was. Then he would slowly stand up, pushing his knee back into place.

In Spartanburg, South Carolina, Dan knocked on the door of a large stone building. The door was opened by a tall man with a big mustache. Close behind the man stood a black bear. It stared over the man's shoulder at Dan.

Dan explained that he was a surveyor and wanted to go to the roof of the building. "Why, sure," the man said. He turned to the bear. "Get out of the way, Henry," he said.

The bear moved away. Dan went into the house and out into a large courtyard. A pack of foxhounds rushed up to play around him. On every side there were cages for many different kinds of animals. Inside the cages were foxes, raccoons, wildcats, squirrels, and rabbits. Dan was delighted with the animals. After a while, he came down from the roof, his drawings finished.

"Would you like to see my chickens?" the man asked.

"What kind of chickens?"

"I'll call them," the man said. "Here, chick-chick-chick!"

From all over the courtyard, birds came flying and running. There were beautiful purple gallinules, wood ducks, doves, grouse, and a whole family of quail.

"When I was a boy," Dan said, "I had all kinds of pets. But you've got a whole zoo."

Not all the animals Dan met in his work were as friendly as these. Once in St. Louis he entered the courtyard of a factory, on his way to the roof. It was a Saturday afternoon, and no one was in sight. Suddenly four huge Great Dane dogs came rushing at him. Their mouths were open, their teeth flashing.

Dan knew that these dogs had been trained to attack. They would kill him if he tried to run. He knew also that dogs will rarely bite a person who stands perfectly still and faces them. So Dan stood without moving as two of the dogs jumped at him. They put their feet on his shoulders. Their open mouths were close to his face.

"Good dogs," Dan said, keeping his voice steady. "Good dogs. I don't want to steal anything, fellows." He kept talking while the giant dogs held him with their feet. The other two circled close around him.

It seemed to Dan that he stood there for hours. Finally a watchman came out of the building. He called the dogs off. Dan went on to the roof and drew his map.

# 6

# A New Career

Dan was 28 years old when he visited
New York City for the first time. He went
walking along Broadway to see the sights.

It was early morning, but the sidewalks
were already crowded. Everybody seemed
to be in a great hurry. There were no
automobiles then, but the streets were
jammed with horse-drawn trucks, wagons,
and carriages. Some of the trucks were so
big that it took four or even six horses to

pull them. A wagon selling ice moved along the rough street. Boys ran beside it and jumped on back of it to steal bits of ice.

At one corner a policeman was helping women and children to cross the street. Dan saw no need to wait for the policeman. He started to cross alone. Several women and children joined him.

Suddenly a big two-horse truck came toward them. Dan could have run, but he wanted to help the people with him. He stood still and held up his hand for the truck to stop. Instead, the driver kept on coming toward him. The front of the wagon hit Dan in the ribs.

Dan caught the horses by the reins and stopped them. He shouted at the driver, "Why are you trying to run over these women? I ought to take that wagon away from you!"

"Try it!" the driver yelled. Ready to fight, he started to get down from the wagon.

Just then the policeman came up. "Get back on your wagon," he told the driver. "Now back it up so these ladies can pass." Then he turned to Dan. "You must be new in the city?"

"I am."

"Well, from now on don't try to direct traffic. Leave that to the police." Then the policeman took Dan to the sidewalk as if he were a small boy.

Dan's brother Frank was an artist like his father. He had a studio in New York. Dan went there to visit him. Dan showed Frank some of the pictures he had painted in his spare time as a surveyor.

While they looked at the pictures, the publisher of a magazine came in. He, too, looked at the pictures. "Some of these are very good," he said. "I could use this one of fishes to illustrate a story in my magazine." He turned to Dan. "Will you take $25 for it?"

"You bet I will," Dan said.

With the money in his pocket, Dan went to the headquarters of the map and publishing company he worked for. He said to the owner, "I won't be back to work for a while. I'm going to take a vacation and paint pictures."

Dan's "vacation" lasted the rest of his life. It was far more fun to paint pictures than to draw maps. From that time on, Dan worked as an artist.

Dan knew that if he was going to be a successful artist, he would need more training. He joined the Art Students' League, where he could study at night. During the day he worked for a store, drawing pictures for its catalog. He drew

pictures of everything from hats and coats to tables and chairs.

This was good training, but the pictures Dan most wanted to paint were of the outdoors. Although he worked in New York City, his home was on Long Island. Here he spent all his spare time, walking in the woods or sailing. He drew pictures of sailboats, birds, and wild animals.

Dan soon began to sell more and more pictures to magazines. Then he began to write stories about the outdoors to tell about his pictures. Sometimes these stories sold to magazines; sometimes they didn't.

One winter day Dan was hurrying to his studio in New York when he passed a group of boys in ragged clothes huddled together on the cold sidewalk. They had nothing to do and no place to go.

Dan walked on to his studio, but he could not forget the boys. In his office he walked back and forth, thinking of his own happy childhood. In Covington even the poorest boys could have fun. They had been able to enjoy the outdoors. They fished and swam in the rivers and roamed the hills. "All boys need to learn about nature," Dan thought.

Suddenly he stood still. "That's what I'll try to do with my pictures and stories," he said aloud. "I'll try to help all boys understand and enjoy the outdoors!"

# 7

# Mark Twain and the *Connecticut Yankee*

From that time on, most of the stories and books that Dan wrote were for boys. One of the books, which is still popular today, is called the *American Boys' Handybook: What to Do and How to Do It*. Others included the *American Boys' Book of Wild Animals* and the *American Boys' Book of Signs, Signals, and Symbols*. In these he told of games boys could play and how to make things like small boats and blowguns, kites and fishing tackle.

Often Dan went on long trips to the West or to the Canadian woods. Then he came back to write about tracking wild animals and how to tell one bird from another. He built his own log cabin in the Pennsylvania mountains. Then he wrote, explaining to boys how they could build outdoor shelters.

On his trips into the wilderness, Dan saw how the nation's forests were being cut down. Factories dumped their wastes into clean rivers and polluted them. Dan began to work for new laws to protect the forests and streams. He made many speeches asking the government to pass laws to set aside land for parks where wild animals would be protected. He fought to stop greedy hunters from killing off birds and animals.

Even though he was grown, Dan still kept pets. One of these was a dog named

Monad. Dan taught Monad how to sneeze and how to close a door. When a friend would come to Dan's studio and leave the door open, Dan would give a signal. The dog would begin to sneeze.

Dan would ask Monad, "Are you catching a cold?" Monad would sneeze again.

"Then go close the door," Dan would order. And while the visitor watched in surprise, Monad would get up and close the door.

Once, one of Dan's friends gave him a snake. It was seven feet long, but it was harmless. Dan put the snake in his overcoat pocket to take it home. Dan was seated on the ferryboat to Long Island, reading a newspaper. Suddenly the woman sitting next to him screamed. She jumped up and ran to the other end of the boat. A man got up and walked quickly away too, then another.

At first Dan could not understand what was happening. Then he looked down and saw that the huge snake had crawled half out of his pocket. Dan put the snake back, but no one returned to sit beside him.

One day Dan was in his studio when a stranger entered. "My name is Fred Hall," he said. "I'm a partner in publishing with Mark Twain."

Mark Twain was the most famous writer in America. Two of his books were *The Adventures of Tom Sawyer* and *The Adventures of Huckleberry Finn*. These were both wonderful stories about boys' adventures that both young people and adults could enjoy.

"Mr. Twain has seen your drawings in a magazine," Fred Hall said. "Now he has written a new book called *A Connecticut Yankee in King Arthur's Court*. He would like you to illustrate it."

"I'd be honored to do so," Dan said.

Dan read the manuscript three times. The story was about a nineteenth century American who mysteriously found himself living in the time of King Arthur. Each time Dan read the story, he liked it better. He went to call on Mark Twain. He asked the author if he had any suggestions about the pictures.

Mark Twain was a tall, thin man with deep lines in his face. His thick hair and his bushy eyebrows were just turning gray. "Mr. Beard," he said, "if a publisher comes to me and asks me to write a story for him, I'll do it. But if he tries to tell me *how* to write it, then he'd better write it himself." Mark Twain took a long pull on his corncob pipe and blew out a cloud of smoke. "You're the artist, Mr. Beard. I'm not going to tell you *how* to draw your pictures."

During the next few months, Dan worked night and day on the pictures for Mark Twain's book. When finally Twain saw them, he was delighted. He sat down and wrote Dan a note.

. . . There are a hundred artists who could have illustrated any other of my books, but only one who could illustrate this one. It was a lucky day I went netting for lightning bugs and caught a meteor. Live forever.

From this time on, as long as Mark Twain lived, he and Dan were friends.

# 8

# Beatrice

After *Connecticut Yankee*, Dan Beard illustrated another book for Mark Twain. It was called *Tom Sawyer Abroad*. Twain told a publisher, "Dan Beard is the only man who can correctly illustrate my stories. He not only shows the story, he shows my thoughts."

One day Dan was walking with a group of friends near his home on Long Island. A yellow cart pulled by a shaggy pony

came by. Dan stopped walking to stare at the girl in the cart. He thought he had never seen a girl so pretty.

"Hello, Bea," said one of Dan's friends. The girl waved and drove on.

Dan turned to his friend. "Who is she?"

"Her name's Beatrice Jackson."

"Well," Dan said, "it's going to be Mrs. Dan Beard. I want you to introduce us."

Beatrice Jackson lived on the other side of a small bay from Dan's home. To see her, Dan often rowed across the water in his small boat. One day he was halfway across when a sudden storm came up. The waves got bigger, and the wind blew harder. Finally the small boat turned over, and Dan was thrown into the water.

Dan was a good swimmer. Even so, he was too far from shore to swim. His boat still floated, so he held on to it.

The storm passed; the wind and rain

ended. The captain of a passing steamboat saw Dan and stopped. A ladder was let down, and Dan climbed on board. "You're safe now," the captain said. "I'll take you to New York."

"I don't want to go to New York," Dan said, pointing across the water. "I've got a girl who lives over there."

"I can't take you over there," the captain said.

Another small boat was sailing beside the steamer now. "Thanks for picking me up," Dan said to the captain. "I'm going to see my girl." He dived over the side of the steamer and swam to the small boat. "How about taking me across the bay?" he asked.

"Sure," the man said. "Climb on board."

An hour later Dan rang Beatrice's doorbell. "I'm late," he told her, laughing, "and a little wet. But I got here."

Not long after this, Dan and Beatrice were married. Dan was 44 years old, his bride much younger. Beatrice loved the outdoors almost as much as Dan did. They spent their honeymoon in the log cabin that Dan had built in the Pennsylvania mountains. They fished and swam in Big Tink Pond nearby.

Then Dan had to go to the Kentucky backwoods to illustrate a book about that area. Later he went to the Canadian forests to draw pictures of lumbermen. Beatrice went with him and often gave him ideas for his pictures.

In time they had two children—a boy and a girl. The children came to enjoy vacations at the cabin as much as their parents.

# 9

# The Sons of Daniel Boone

As Dan grew older, he worked not only as an artist and writer, but also as the editor of a magazine called *Recreation*. This magazine was read chiefly by hunters and fishermen, but Dan also wanted to interest boys. He talked things over with the magazine's business manager, Bill Annis.

"I'd like to do something," Dan said, "that would help boys learn to enjoy the outdoors. At the same time, they would learn how important it is to keep our forests from being cut down and the wildlife from being killed off."

"When you were a boy, how did you get interested in nature?" Annis asked.

"Covington was a small town then," Dan said. "There was a gang of us called the Boone Scouts, and—" Suddenly Dan jumped to his feet. "That's it!" he cried. "My gang had great fun pretending to be the sons of Daniel Boone. While we tried to be like him, we learned a lot about nature and the outdoors. I want to start the Boone Scouts all over again!"

Dan wrote an article for his magazine. In it he said:

I propose that we form a society to be called "The Sons of Daniel Boone." American and Canadian

boys will unite in one brotherhood
to protect our brothers in fur,
feathers, scales, and bark.

Our object will be: the study of
woodcraft; outdoor sports and fun;
along with serious work to save
and protect our native plants,
birds, and beasts.

Each club, Dan said, would be called a
fort.

Dan wanted famous Americans to help
get the Sons of Daniel Boone started. He
went to Washington to call on President
Theodore Roosevelt.

President Roosevelt was an enthusiastic
outdoorsman. As a young man, he had
been a cowboy, a big game hunter, and
a soldier. As president, he had done a lot
for conservation, saving wildlife and the

wilderness. "I've read your books and enjoyed your pictures," he told Dan. "You are doing wonderful work. How can I be of help?"

Dan explained his plan. "To make the organization well known," he said, "I need the help of famous men. John Muir and John Burroughs, the great naturalists, have joined. So has Buffalo Bill."

"Bully!" Roosevelt banged the desk with his fist. "Who else do you need?"

"I'd like somebody to represent the sea."

"Admiral Dewey," Roosevelt replied. "I'll write a note to him. Who else?"

Dan grinned. "I'd like you to join too, Mr. President."

Roosevelt roared with laughter. "The way you put it, I can't refuse."

Before long, boys all over the country heard about the Sons of Daniel Boone. They wrote to Dan asking how to start their own forts. They asked what work they could do to "protect our brothers in fur, feathers, scales, and bark." Sometimes Dan answered as many as 50 letters a day.

Very soon the Sons of Daniel Boone became the biggest boys' club in America.

# 10

# The Boy Scouts of America

It was a hot June day in 1910. Dan walked slowly along East 28th Street. It was in a poor section of New York. The dirty street was crowded not only with horse-drawn carts and wagons, but also with children. Some tried to play stickball while running between the wagons. Some played hopscotch on the hot sidewalk. Some just sat in the shadow of doorways with nothing to do.

Dan was 60 years old now. He was just as lean and straight as ever, his face deeply browned by the sun. "Some of these city youngsters have never seen a lake or forest," he thought. "Perhaps this new plan will help them to know and love nature. If it will, then I'll do what I can to help." He turned away from the street and went into a tall building.

Here waiting for him were some of the most important men in the country. They had come to talk about a new organization for boys which had been incorporated several months earlier by William Boyce, an American newspaper publisher, and several other men. It was called the Boy Scouts of America. William Boyce had modeled the new group after the British Boy Scouts, an organization founded by Robert Baden-Powell, a British general. Now Boyce wanted to interest the leaders of other boys' groups in the new organization. He hoped that men like Dan Beard and Ernest Thompson Seton would help the Boy Scouts to become a strong organization in the United States.

About the same time that Dan Beard had started the Sons of Daniel Boone, Ernest Thompson Seton had formed another organization. It was called the Woodcraft Indians. Seton, like Dan, was a writer, artist, and naturalist who loved the outdoors. His Woodcraft Indians had many of the same interests held by the Sons of Daniel Boone. These two groups were the largest boys' clubs in America. There were also many smaller ones.

Now Dan Beard, Ernest Seton, Boyce, and other leaders were meeting to decide an important question. Should these different groups join together? If so, how should they be organized?

"There's only one important question," Dan Beard told the men. "What is best for the boys? I'm proud of the Sons of Daniel Boone and the work I have done with them. But one large national organization probably can do more for boys than several smaller ones. If so, I'll vote for the Sons of Daniel Boone to join. The new group can be called the Woodcraft Indians or Boy Scouts, or whatever is decided."

"I agree," Ernest Seton said. "Like Dan, I'm proud of my work with the Woodcraft Indians. But I believe one organization would be best for all boys. So I'm willing for the Indians to join."

One by one the others there agreed. So on this hot June day in 1910, many smaller organizations joined to form one large organization. It would still be called the Boy Scouts of America.

Now, would the boys of America be really interested in this new group?

They were interested. From all over the country, letters poured into the one-room headquarters of the new Scouts. Churches wanted to know how to start Boy Scout troops. Questions came from YMCA groups asking how they could help. Civic leaders gave their time. But most of the letters were from boys themselves, thousands of them. How could they start troops? Where could they turn for help?

Dan Beard had never been so busy. He had been named as the National Scout Commissioner. He helped to make the rules for setting up troops. He designed the uniform and the pin the Scouts would wear. To the pin worn by British Boy Scouts, Dan added an eagle for the American Boy Scouts. Proud of his country, Dan wanted to be sure that scouting in America followed American traditions.

When the scouting magazine *Boys' Life* began, Dan wrote articles for every issue. Month after month he wrote about the two things that seemed to him most important. One was how to have fun in the outdoors. The other was conservation —how to save the forests and streams so that other persons could enjoy them later. He told how to build campfires and how to keep these campfires from becoming forest fires. He told how to cut down trees for wigwams and lean-tos. He explained how new trees should be planted so that forests would always be growing.

More than any other one man, Dan Beard came to represent the spirit of scouting in America. From Maine to California the Boy Scouts knew and loved him as Uncle Dan.

# 11

# End of the Trail

Dan's work with the Boy Scouts became even more famous than his books and pictures. All over the country, he helped to start Boy Scout troops. He took boys on camping trips. He taught them how to take care of themselves in the woods. He taught them a love of nature. He gave talks not only to Scouts, but also to grown-ups who wanted to work with and help boys.

In his talks Dan often told about the first Boone Scouts and the hideout on Bank Lick.

"I always remember," he said, "how we boys wondered what had happened to the buffalo. None of us then could believe that the passenger pigeons and the wild parakeets could be killed off. There were too many of them. Yet today there is not a single passenger pigeon or wild parakeet left alive in this country. Many other animals are in danger too. If we don't protect them, they also will disappear."

For his talks Dan often wore a fancy buckskin costume he had designed himself. It had a fringed shirt and a fringed leather jacket. He wore leather boots and a wide-brimmed hat.

One winter night Dan made a speech in New York. The weather was very cold.

Going home, he wore an overcoat that hid his buckskins. It was late, and Dan had to change streetcars in a part of the city where robberies were common. While he waited for the next car, Dan stood close beside a streetlight.

Suddenly four tough-looking men came out of the shadows. They were heading for Dan, wanting to rob him. There was no one else in sight, and Dan had no weapon to protect himself.

Without seeming to hurry, Dan opened his overcoat so the men could see his costume. He put one hand deep in the pocket of his buckskin jacket. Then he faced the would-be robbers and waited.

The men stopped, staring at Dan. Then, suddenly, they disappeared back into the shadows.

When Dan got home, he told his family what had happened. His wife and children began to laugh. "No wonder they ran," his son said. "When they saw your clothes, they probably thought you were Buffalo Bill. They thought you had two six-shooters in your pocket."

Dan was very proud of his children. As they became older, his daughter often helped with his books. His son became a well-known naturalist. He later mapped the swampland called the Everglades in Florida and studied the wildlife there.

Dan himself changed very little as he grew old. There were deep wrinkles in his face, but he was still thin and straight. His eyes were bright, and he always looked as if he was just about to tell a joke.

At 74, Dan went camping with a group of men interested in helping the Scouts. Dan was the oldest man there, but he was one of the youngest in spirit.

"Remember," he told them, "it was God who made the outdoors. . . . Camping is the greatest incentive to go outdoors. But don't fix up a steam-heated apartment with electric lights, warm water, and all that sort of thing and call it a camp. . ."

Beard felt strongly that people could feel close to nature only if they camped out in a very simple manner.

When the first Boy Scout Jamboree was held in the United States, Dan Beard was 87 years old. It was Uncle Dan, as the Scouts of the world knew him, who lit the first campfire. And each night of the Jamboree, Scouts gathered in Uncle Dan's tent to hear him tell stories about the outdoors.

Two years later Dan Beard sat down to write the story of his life. In it he wrote very little about the honors he had received and the important work he had done. Instead, he wrote about the things he remembered and enjoyed the most. He wrote about the Boone Scouts crossing Bank Lick on a grapevine swing, the eggs that had blown up because he forgot to punch a hole in them. Then he told about his love of nature: "especially the primitive wilderness—unmanicured, unshaven, without a haircut." Dan had devoted much of his life to keeping that wilderness unspoiled so that others, too, could enjoy it.

For Dan Beard it was this love of the outdoors that was truly important. This was how he would feel until his death at the age of 91. And this was what he wanted to leave to the Boy Scouts and to all the boys of the world.

# The Silver Crest

# THE
# SILVER CREST

MY RUSSIAN BOYHOOD

## by Kornei Chukovsky

Translated from the Russian by
BEATRICE STILLMAN

Holt, Rinehart and Winston · New York

Library of Congress Cataloging in Publication Data
Chukovskiĭ, Korneĭ Ivanovich, 1882–1969.
The silver crest.

Translation of Serebrǐanyĭ gerb.
SUMMARY:   Relates a young Russian boy's experiences
growing up in Odessa in the 1890's.
[1.   Russia—Fiction]   I.   Title.
PZ7.C4587Si        [Fic]        75-32248
ISBN 0-03-014241-5

# The Silver Crest

# The Gymnasium

This is a true story. It begins in the year 1893 in the
south of Russia, in a seaport town named Odessa. In
those days, the basic school which young people between
the ages of nine and seventeen attended—that is, if their
parents could afford to pay for their tuition, their books
and the special uniforms they had to wear—was called a
gymnasium. Despite its name, a gymnasium was not a
room where sports were performed. It was a strict, demand-
ing school in which the students had to study Latin and
Greek on top of all their other subjects. And, like all
students everywhere, then and now, they often wished
they were somewhere else.

B. S.

# 1

## The Telephone

Zuyev pulled a dozen little pictures of saints out of his schoolbag—copper ones, tin ones, wood and paper ones—spread them out on his desk and began kissing them one after the other, in a business-like way. He didn't skip even one saint, for fear it might get insulted and play some nasty trick on him.

It wasn't for nothing that Zuyev was praying. In another few minutes our class was going to be given a test —a very scary test in dictation—that we had been expecting for eleven days. Eleven days ago our school principal, Mr. Burgmeister, (we called him "Six-Eyes") came into our room clacking his bootheels and read us an announcement in a stern, solemn voice, as if he was reading poetry.

*"The Honorable Trustee of the Educational District,*
*His Excellency*
*Count Nikolai Ferdinandovich von Lustig,*
*will shortly afford our class the honor of a visit,*

*and may perhaps express the desire to attend the Russian lesson during the period of dictation."*

And now the day was here. I felt specially sorry for my best friend, Timosha Makarov, who sat in the row behind me. He was just back in school after being sick with typhoid fever, and he was way behind the rest of us. When I glanced back at him, I saw a look of deathly fear on his freckled face. Poor Timosha! Suddenly I had a brilliant idea.

I was considered the champion dictation taker in our class. I didn't understand it myself. From the age of seven, I could write the most complicated phrases without a mistake. I had a perfect record on commas. In other subjects I wasn't that great, but in Russian I used to get straight 5's (even though right alongside of the 5 they used to put down a 1 on account of my blots). At that time I just couldn't get the hang of writing without blots. After every dictation my fingers would be so smeared up with ink that it looked as if I had dipped them into the inkwell on purpose.

"Timosha—wait a minute—I have it!" I said.

I pulled a kite string out from under my shirt, tied it to my shoe and handed the other end of it to Timosha.

"Tie it on your leg. Make it tight!"

Then, while he was busy tying the knots, I explained the code to him. "If I pull the string once, that means comma. Two pulls is an exclamation mark. Three pulls—question mark. Four pulls is a colon. Get it?"

Timosha nodded cheerfully and tried to tell me something. But he couldn't control his stuttering, so the only thing that came out of his mouth was a little spray of spit.

# The Telephone

Next to Timosha sat a short, curly-haired, quick-moving fellow, Munya Blokhin. Munya dove under the desk to extend the "telephone" line. He wasn't about to let such an opportunity pass him by, no sir! A student who had flunked last year and had to take the whole year over again —Sasha Bugai—was sitting just in back of Timosha. We passed the line on to him too.

Munya pulled a piece of twine out of his pocket and stretched it tight from Timosha to Sasha, who then tied it to his right leg. Next to Bugai was Zuzya Kozelsky, the worst student in our class. He was also a crybaby, a coward and a beggar who always wanted something. If we didn't put him into our telephone system he would start sniveling and whining and give us all away.

Behind Zuzya, way off by the wall in the corner of the room we called "Siberia," were the Babenchikov brothers, famous throughout the school as loafers and louts. Their fists were as heavy as lead weights. We had no choice but to extend our line to them too.

Blokhin coached the signals. "Don't forget, now," he said. "One: comma. Two: exclamation mark. Three: question mark. Four: colon. Got it straight?"

Meanwhile Zuyev, though he went right on crossing himself and mumbling his prayers, watched Munya and me out of the corner of his eye. Suddenly he scooped up all his saints and threw them back into his schoolbag, ripped off a thread from around his neck, got down on his knees under his desk and tied his string to my shoe.

Now the door to our room opened wide, and in walked . . . not our principal, Mr. Burgmeister, and not His Excellency Count von Lustig, whose name they had been scaring us with for eleven days, but some wooden-looking stranger with a face like a hatchet. Without a word, he started at once to read the dictation aloud.

Did my right leg go to work! The whole time the dictation was going on, I jerked and jerked till I couldn't see straight.

> On that day (jerk!), when valiant Igor (jerk!), leading the troops out of the forests and swamps (jerk!), noticed that in the field (jerk!), where the enemy was standing (jerk!), an ominous cloud of dust had risen (jerk!), he said (jerk! jerk! jerk! jerk!): "How glorious to die for one's fatherland (jerk! jerk!)!

Our desks were shaking as if they had convulsions. I kept sending signals to Zuyev, Timosha and Munya. Timosha passed them on to Sasha, and Munya to Zuzya Kozelsky and the Babenchikov brothers.

When the dictation came to an end, the wooden stranger with the hatchet face took our notebooks away from us and carried them away with him to God knows where. As it later turned out, he was an important official from Count von Lustig's office.

And did they ever thank me, the seven fellows I rescued from disaster! Zuzya Kozelsky promised me one of his pigeons and the Babenchikov brothers offered me a whole capful of raisins. Their father owned the best sweetshop in town on Ekaterinskaya Street, where he sold dates, figs, coconut and halvah.

The next week the wooden stranger came to us again, together with our form master, Mr. Fleurov. He announced that, by order of the Honorable Trustee of the Educational District, His Excellency Count von Lustig, the Commission for Verification of Educational Progress had examined the notebooks in which our dictations were written down, and that the Commission had taken notice of a certain very peculiar thing. . . .

The stranger started riffling through the notebooks. "Let us, for example, take the case of Zuyev and Kozelsky. Might I invite them up to the blackboard?"

Zuyev and Kozelsky ran happily up to the blackboard and put on an air of dignified modesty, waiting to be praised. The stranger looked at them and suddenly, to the amazement of the class, he smiled just like a real live human being. And then he turned to the blackboard and wrote the following sentence on it with chalk:

> On that day when: valiant Igor leading? the troops out of the forests and swamps noticed that in the field where? the enemy, was standing an ominous cloud, of dust!? had risen?

"That is the way third-year student Kozelsky wrote his dictation. For such a dictation a mark of 1 is too high. We hereby give Kozelsky a zero, just like Zuyev."

We all burst out laughing, and someone whistled. The stranger tapped his wooden finger on the lectern and said—now without a trace of a smile—"But there are some students among you who are unworthy even to receive a zero. They are Maxim and Alexander Babenchikov. Alexander Babenchikov wrote down his dictation like this." And he wrote the following on the board:

> On that day when valiant Igor lead,ing the troops out of the for?ests and sw,amps no:ticed that in the field where the en,emy was standing an ominous? cloud of dust had! risen he said how glor,ious to die: for one's Fath?erland?

· 5 ·

The cause of this disaster was—me. I gave the signals as I wrote. And it seems that I wrote more slowly than the rest. On top of that, the blots kept holding me up. By the time I got around to the third or fourth word, the other fellows were on their seventh, maybe their ninth. Trusting blindly in my telephone, the boys sitting the farthest away from me stopped using their brains altogether. Operating by signals alone, they were ready to put a comma inside of every word even if it cut the word in half— something the stupidest moron on earth wouldn't do.

After that day was over it was a long time before I could cough, or laugh, or sneeze, or sigh. That was how much my ribs hurt after my "pals" (mostly the Babenchikov brothers) expressed their gratitude to me for my services. It was no use at all trying to make them understand that even the greatest invention on earth isn't perfect the first time it's tried.

It was four days before I was in condition to come back to school. By that time, the rumors about our telephone system were buzzing through all the classrooms and corridors. But Six-Eyes preferred to keep up the pretense that he knew nothing about it. Otherwise he would have been forced to punish Zuyev and the Babenchikov brothers, who were special pets of his, for certain reasons of his own.

Soon after that our final exams began. I forgot all about the "telephone." But two years later, when I was in the fifth-year class, I had occasion to think of it again. At that time I was overtaken by a new calamity, and I took a punishment so terrible that I will never forget the "telephone" to the end of my days.

It all started with our school priest.

# 2

## Yes-Yes-Yes!

The priest's name was Father Melety. He tried to be kind but he didn't succeed very well, because he got insulted easily. He would be holding a conversation with us in a sweet, low voice and telling us that we must love our enemies as tenderly as our friends, when suddenly his face would turn green with anger.

"How dare you laugh at me! Munya Blokhin, why are you sniggering?"

"I'm not sniggering, Father!"

"You are! You are sniggering! All of you there in the back row are sniggering! Kozelsky isn't sniggering! Zuyev isn't sniggering! Babenchikov isn't sniggering! But you in the back row are sniggering! Why are you sniggering?"

"Father, we aren't sniggering!"

He was always a little absentminded during the lesson period. He would gather his whole beard together into his fist, fix his eyes on a single point and repeat dreamily, "Yes-yes-yes-yes-yes!" Even while someone was answering a lesson question, he would look right through him, and, gazing off into the distance, confirming his own private thoughts, he'd say disconnectedly, "Yes-yes-yes!"

One day it came into my head to count how many times he'd say the word "yes" in one lesson. I started dipping my finger into my mouth and writing on my desk with my wet finger, 30 . . . 40 . . . 48 . . . 53 . . . 60 . . . .

Sitting next to me was Grishka Zuyev. At first he watched my calculations with no interest at all, but things had become so unbearably boring in class that he couldn't stand it. Zuyev spit on his finger and he too started covering his side of the desk with figures.

Little by little we both got carried away. Every time the absentminded priest repeated "yes-yes-yes" we would erase the old number with the palms of our hands and hurry to write in the new total. Each fresh "yes" gave us as much pleasure as winning a game.

But soon I realized that Zuyev was starting to cheat. Instead of 211 he put down 290, and then changed it to 320 right away. I was furious at this gypping. In my anger I reached over to his half of the desk, wiped out the false count and put in the right one: 211.

Now Zuyev was angry. His eyes bulged and his fat face turned red.

Suddenly we heard Father Melety's voice.

"Zuyev—and you, there—what's your name? Come on now. Repeat what I just said."

It was really a very strange thing. We were paying very close attention to the lesson. We had to be, in order to catch each "yes." But now it turned out that "yes-yes-yes" was all we had heard. Because it isn't water, after all, that a fisherman catches in his net—it's fish.

Embarrassed, we stood there and mumbled something. Zuyev got away with it. His big head, round as a watermelon, leaned now to the right, now to the left, giving him the look of a downcast sinner suffering the torments of repentance.

Father Melety was pleased with this penitent pose. Father Melety loved weeping, submissive, humiliated boys. He narrowed one eye and admired the suffering Zuyev the way an artist admires a painting. And said benignly, "Yes-yes-yes!"

"Four hundred and twelve," Zuyev whispered to me while maintaining his martyr's pose.

"That's a lie!" I exploded. "It's not four hundred and twelve, it's two hundred and fourteen!"

My voice was high-pitched, and the word "lie" rang out like a shot.

Father Melety tousled his beard. "Step up to the blackboard this minute," he said, "and tell the entire class the reason for your indecent howl."

Then he added, "Yes!"

This last "yes" sent me into a fit of laughing.

"You are sniggering!" Father Melety shouted. "You are happy to be corrupting pious Zuyev with your vile behavior!"

At that the whole class burst out laughing. "Pious" Zuyev was a notorious foul-mouth who swore like a trooper.

Wanting to show Father Melety that I wasn't nearly as bad as he thought, that I wouldn't dream of corrupting pious Zuyev, I blurted out the truth.

"You see, Father," I said politely and confidentially, "you have this habit of saying 'yes-yes-yes.' So I thought I would count up how many times in one lesson—"

He didn't let me finish. Grabbing his beard, he began to pull hairs out of it furiously. The angrier he was, the more mercilessly he always tore at his own beard. And he never calmed down until he had pulled two or three hairs out of it.

This time he tore out ten. Then he laid them down one next to the other on the black cover of our class record book, blew on them with all his might and began to speak very slowly, in a muffled, barely audible voice (his voice always lowered to a whisper when he was truly furious).

He said he was a servant at God's altar, yes-yes-yes! And would not permit—yes-yes-yes!—any little pipsqueak —yes-yes-yes!—to . . . He talked for a long time. And in the same whisper—which seemed worse to me than any shout—he ordered me to get out of the class immediately.

I left the room and stood near the door.

Father Melety went on talking about my evil deeds and called me some kind of "onager." What an onager was I didn't know at that time, and I quietly moved out into the hall.

The recess was about to begin. Plates and glasses started clinking at the end of the hall. Our school watchman, Pushkin, was setting out milk bottles, sausage, sandwiches and pirozhki on a long table covered with a dirty cloth.

I found four kopecks in my pocket. I rushed over to Pushkin and bought a pirozhok—a meat dumpling. The minute I stuffed it into my mouth the bell rang. Students started pouring out of all the classrooms. There was Father

Melety, fingering the silver cross on his chest and striding toward the teachers' room.

I decided to ask his forgiveness.

To tell the truth, I didn't need it for myself. But on Rybnaya Street, in an annex of the Makry house, lived a sad, quiet woman—my mother; and I knew that my quarrel with the priest would be a great tragedy for her. Every time I got into some kind of trouble at school, my mother would take a towel, dip it in vinegar and wrap it around her head. That meant she had a headache and would be lying in bed without moving, half-dead, with darkened eyelids, for days on end.

I was ready to do anything in the world to make my mother's head stop aching. And that was why I ran after the priest begging him, with tears in my eyes, "Father, please forgive me!"

But my mouth was full of food, so it came out like "Fada, pwa fgie ma!"

He turned to look at me. Suddenly, his pale, thin lips twisted in a look of horror. "You—you—you!" he exclaimed, choking with anger, and grabbed me by the shoulder.

I stared at him. All at once I realized what had happened. The dumpling was filled with meat, and today was Friday! Father Melety had told us a thousand times that Christians must not eat meat on Wednesdays and Fridays, especially during Lent, since God would be offended if during those days we ate even the smallest piece of beef.

I didn't put too much stock in this. Wouldn't God find it boring to look inside every schoolboy's mouth? But Father Melety assured us that it was so. And woe betide

the impious one who today—on a Friday!—had the gall
to stand in front of him with a meat dumpling in his
mouth, on purpose to make a mockery of him, yes-yes-yes!

An unchewed lump of the criminal dumpling stuck in
my throat. I understood that now there was no forgiveness
for me and there would not be any. But still I went on
repeating mechanically, "Father, please forgive me!"

But I could see from his tightly drawn brows and by his
twisted lower lip that my case was lost.

"As a Christian," he said, "I forgive you. As your spirit-
ual father, I pray for you. But as your teacher of religious
law, I am obliged to punish you. For your own salvation."

A crowd started to collect around us. I saw Zuyev,
standing behind Father Melety and sucking a chicken
leg, with the sweetest smile on his face. His fleshy, old-
womanish face was greasy with chicken fat.

Suddenly Father Melety bowed to someone. Our school
principal, Six-Eyes himself, was walking toward us, clacking the heels of his elegant little boots. He turned to me
and said in his mock-joking way, "I've been hearing things
about you, yes, I've heard about your artistic exploits!
Would you be kind enough to pay me the honor of a visit
—in the sobbing room—*right now.*"

# 3

# Zuzya

The principal wore a pince-nez on top of his eyeglasses. That was why we called him Six-Eyes. But his real name was Burgmeister. Like many other Russified Germans, he expressed himself in an exaggeratedly "Russian" way and loved to use peasant language and homely phrases —words he considered deeply Russian. He was a master of this style. But for some reason his language made me sick.

Whenever he bawled us out he would get drunk on his own flights of fancy and go on and on. Even when he was alone with some little first-year kid, he would orate as if he was standing before an audience of thousands.

When I came near his office door I saw that one "sobber" was already inside. It was Zuzya Kozelsky, frightened to death, with his face all swollen from crying. Six-Eyes had advanced on him so hard with the physical force of his body that he seemed to be trying to push Zuzya right through the wall. The miserable kid was pressed flat against the wall, not only with his back but also with his head and heels. But since the wall was made of stone, Six-Eyes could go on haranguing him as long as he felt like it.

"Do I dare believe my eyes?" he declaimed, stepping back one pace and waving a battered notebook in time to his words. "Does my vision betray me? Is this a mirage? Is it a specter? Can it be you, Kozelsky, that very same Kozelsky who only last year was the pride of his preceptors, the consolation of his parents, the joy of his brothers, the moral support of his family . . ."

He could go on like that forever, imitating the great orators of old. He tormented Kozelsky for no less than thirty minutes, and it wasn't until the half hour was almost up that I realized what his crime was.

It was no petty crime.

It all began with the fact that Zuzya had been given no less than two 1's that week, in what subjects I don't remember. These 1's had been put down in his school notebook by the form master himself, Mr. Fleurov. And Zuzya was supposed to show his father these marks and get his signature under them. But since Zuzya's father had threatened to give him a beating the first time he brought home a bad mark, Zuzya took the advice of his pal Tuntin. He wrote over the numbers in his notebook so that the 1's came out looking like 4's. This was a simple enough trick. Zuzya's father didn't notice anything wrong and signed his name to the forged 4's with much satisfaction.

But Zuzya wasn't very experienced at this. When the

time came to change the 4's back into 1's and hand the book over to the form master, he erased the extra pen strokes so clumsily that instead of 1's he got two holes in the paper.

What to do now? Once the teacher got a look at those two holes, Zuzya might just as well forget about going home. There was nothing to do but cover up all traces of the crime. So it was that the evening before, acting again on the advice of that same pal, Tuntin, Zuzya made up his mind to bury his 1's in a grave from which they could never be resurrected. He made his way secretly into our gymnasium yard, dug a hole under an acacia tree (not a very deep hole, because the ground was hard and flinty) and there buried his school notebook forever.

He was perfectly sure (and Tuntin helped convince him of this) that as soon as he made the announcement that his notebook had disappeared he would be given a new notebook right away, without any 1's or 2's marked in it, without blots and smears and teachers' comments. And then he would begin a new, fresh, beautiful life.

There was only one witness to the crime, the New-foundland dog, Achilles, who belonged to Six-Eyes. Every Sunday morning the principal, with an unlighted cigar in his mouth, took Achilles for a walk along the seashore. Throughout the secret burial of the notebook Achilles gazed at Zuzya with kindly eyes.

But this kindly animal, who wagged his tail in such a friendly way, betrayed Zuzya like the lowest traitor. The moment Zuzya's work was finished and he went away happy, the dog dug up the burial mound with his kindly paws and grabbed the buried notebook with his teeth.

Without the least understanding of the immorality of his behavior, he ran straight to Six-Eyes and dropped his find at his master's feet.

And now that very book, smeared with earth, battered and torn, was located in our principal's left hand. Six-Eyes was waving it in front of Zuzya's nose and practically threatening the criminal with Siberia. I knew that the same ordeal was in store for me: a whole hour of being pressed against the wall and listening to Six-Eyes deliver his monologue.

But, as it turned out, things were even worse than that.

The moment Zuzya left, Six-Eyes hurled his whole stock of thunder-and-lightning bolts at me. He said I was the biggest evildoer on the face of the earth, that I had mocked the rites of the church, corrupted honest Zuyev, schemed to construct a whole rigging of lines to signal my schoolmates during the dictation period (that was when he harked back to the old history of the "telephone") and *deliberately* given them false signals, so that they would get zeros. . . .

"Deliberately?"

"Deliberately! *Deliberately*! And you think I don't know about it?" he shouted, advancing still closer on top of me. "You think I don't know that it was you who egged Kozelsky on to change his 1's into 4's and then bury his notebook under a tree?"

"Who—me?"

I felt as if someone had hit me between the eyes with a whip. I shouted in the principal's face that he was telling lies, lies, lies. And when he tried to go on with his speech, I let out a yell and covered up my ears with my hands so as not to hear any more of that unbearable lying.

*Zuzya*

Six-Eyes grabbed my hands and tried to tear them away from my ears, but I resisted desperately. Finally he managed to get possession of one ear, and he yelled into it without any further flourishes or eloquent phrases that he was going to report my defiant behavior to the School Board, and that until that body pronounced sentence on me, he was suspending me from school for two weeks. And tomorrow, namely, Saturday—well, no—Monday— my mother was to come to see him. My mother, who— well, he was going to have a personal talk with her . . . and let her know that she had only herself to blame for all this, because she didn't know how to bring up her son properly.

# 4

# The Sad Road Home

When I walked home from school that day I was worn out. I remember a neighbor's kid, Vanya Aligeraki, running up and starting to show me a big glass jar with some kind of a whiskered, sand-colored fish in it that he had caught with his hands. It took all my self-control to keep from taking that jar and dashing it against a rock.

As I turned into Kanatnaya Street a cart was rolling past, loaded to the top with reed. It was the first time in my life I ever let a cart like that go by without grabbing a piece of reed. For me, any piece of reed was a real find. You could make a lance out of it and do battle in the back courts with the army of Vaska Pechonkin the blacksmith. You could carve a fife out of it and pipe under Crazy Benka's window till Benka himself jumped out, yelling at you, "Show-off!" You could make a kite frame out of it and fly it so high that Pechonkin, who was the champion kite flyer on our street, would be jealous.

But today, although the street was deserted and I could easily have snitched not one but several pieces of reed, I didn't even try to approach the cart.

On the corner of Kanatnaya and Rybnaya I discovered a tin box right at my feet. Any other day I would have kicked it with the tip of my boot, sending it bouncing and clattering along the cobblestones right up to the entrance gate of my house, and then I would have hidden it somewhere in the trash pile, so as to chase it back to school the next day. That was one of the favorite amusements in my life. But now I kicked it off to the side and hunched myself over. Ever since I was a little kid I've been in the habit of stooping over. When some misfortune came my way, I would bend over like a question mark. Because of this, the boys on my street called me "Gawky."

If my mother would give me a good scolding or even a beating, it would make things better. But she wouldn't say a word. She would only fall into bed. Her face would turn yellow, her eyelids would darken, her head would start aching and her life would come to a stop for several days.

And what would happen to her on Monday? Exhausted, she would rise from her bed. Barely able to drag one leg after the other, she would go and pay Six-Eyes a visit. He would exhaust his entire stock of high-sounding phrases for her benefit, would tell her that her son was a good-for-nothing and that there was only one career open to him: to become a tramp.

My mother was a very brave woman. She had only one

fear in her life: that I might for some reason be expelled from the gymnasium. That was something she feared more than death itself.

I couldn't stand the thought of going home. I stood in front of a big shop, V.I. and M.I. Sarafanov Brothers' Gastronomic Delicacies, and slowly inspected all the sausages, olives, caviar, smoked sturgeon and cheeses in their window. That store was like some splendid palace to me. Sometimes I myself was a customer there. Whenever my mother had the money for it, I used to run to Sarafanov's with a half-ruble coin and, feeling like a very important personage, say "A quarter of a pound of ham and a quarter of a pound of butter!"

The clerk would ask respectfully, "What else would you like?"

And I would answer, "Nothing at the moment."

"Then kindly go to the cashier!" the clerk would say.

I wanted to find out someday what caviar tasted like. People said that caviar was something unbelievably delicious, but so expensive that only generals and ministers could afford to eat it. Or rich people like Madam Shershenevich. It would be interesting to know—did Six-Eyes eat caviar? Of course he did. In gigantic spoonfuls.

Normally when I was standing in front of that store I would be gripped by a fierce appetite. I would feel as if I could swallow up the whole window. But today even the caviar had no attraction for me, even though the only thing I had eaten all day was that damned meat dumpling.

I walked on, stooped as if my schoolbag was full of bricks. A gymnasium student passed by, an eighth-year man named Ludwig Meier. We called him "Spinoza." Frowning, his puffy face immobile, he was holding an open book under his chin and reading while he walked. The boys who ran around with Vaska Pechonkin's gang were throwing trash under his feet, hoping he would trip and drop his book.

But even as he tripped, he went on reading. He read all the time and everywhere, in the most peculiar places— the bakery, the bathhouse, the cemetery. And therefore I considered him the most educated and most intelligent person on earth.

If things had been different, I would certainly have taken off after the kids in Pechonkin's gang. But today I didn't care and went on walking, rubbing salt in my own wounds.

Would Mama ever believe that none of it, *none of it,* was my fault? And even if it was my fault, well, maybe just a teeny little. . . . What in the heck ever possessed me to go get mixed up with Father Melety? But could they really kick you out of the gymnasium for a little thing like that?

Now I was passing by Madam Shershenevich's house. It was three stories high, with little balconies and peeling plaster statues. And there was Madam Shershenevich, taking her lapdogs out for a walk. She looked like a lapdog herself—tiny and jumpy, with lots of little curls all over her head. The earrings in her ears were as big and round as bagels.

"Hello there!" she shouted to me. "Why are you stooped over like that? You're not seventy years old yet!"

She didn't have the slightest interest in me. The reason she was shouting so playfully and in such a ringing tone of voice was only because there was a group of lieutenants and cadets collected on the other side of the street, near the gates of the Army barracks. They were the reason she was walking her dogs. The cadets and lieutenants shouted pleasantries to her from across the street, admired her beauty and invited her to go dancing. And she laughed trillingly and slyly, looking not at them but at her lapdogs.

# 5

# Top Hat

Yes, it's true. My mother is a very brave woman. She isn't afraid of anybody in the world, except Six-Eyes. One time, a burglar broke into Madam Shershenevich's apartment in the middle of the night, and boy! did my mother settle his hash!

It was three years ago. Madam Shershenevich wasn't at home at the time. She and her husband had gone away to Kiev, and her apartment was empty. She asked my mother to watch it for her, and the three of us, my mother, my older sister Marusya and I, moved in there for the summer.

The lapdogs lived with us. They had to have special food, and we were always making trips to the market to get it for them. We also had to take care of her plants and flowers. And Madam Shershenevich had an awful lot of plants. We were supposed to water them every morning and every night. We also had to exterminate whole battalions of bedbugs, which nested all over Madam

Shershenevich's apartment—in the couches, behind the wallpaper, inside the divans, even in back of the mirror and picture frames. This work took up all my mother's time.

One stifling moonlight night my mother was awakened by the barking of a dog. In the dining room, which looked out on the street, all four of Madam Shershenevich's lapdogs were yapping. Mama ran into the room half-dressed and saw a man's figure standing on the windowsill, surrounded by fuchsias, oleanders and figs.

She took a good hard look at him. He was a puny ragamuffin of about seventeen, maybe younger, bedraggled, bareheaded and shivering. He had climbed up to the second floor (most likely by way of the downspout) and got all tangled up in the thicket of plants. The dogs were arranged around him in a semicircle, defending Madam Shershenevich's household with so much zeal that they were hoarse from yapping.

When he saw my mother, this ragamuffin grabbed up a flower pot from the windowsill and, cursing hoarsely as if he had a cold, threw it at the dogs like a bomb. They set up a yelping and howling and squealing, and for a moment they scattered in all directions. But then they closed in again and started yipping with fresh enthusiasm.

My mother spoke to the burglar in a calm, quiet voice. "You simpleton, you! Who goes out to steal by the light of the moon? And why are you shouting at the top of your voice? You want to bring the whole street here, so they can grab you quicker?"

The thief answered with a flood of curse words. Grabbing the very biggest pot from the windowsill, he aimed it at Mama with all his strength. She bent over lightly and the pot landed in the empty aquarium behind her.

The uproar finally woke me up. I ran into the room, grabbing an iron candlestick just in case (I had been using it the night before to crack nuts on the door threshold). Mama went on talking to the thief the whole time in an even voice, just as if she was reading something out of a book.

"What a lazybones you are. Don't even know how to steal properly. If you had only come to me like a decent fellow, I would have given you some bread and lard."

Not till then did I realize what to do. I ran for the yardkeeper by the back stairs. His door was locked. I pounded on it with my fists and with the iron candlestick. The yardkeeper didn't answer but my knocks were heard in the next apartment, and the orderly who worked for General Eltsov's wife ran out to get the policeman and the guard.

Mama didn't give them a friendly reception. "You're too late. He went that way. . . ." And she pointed in the direction of Old Portofrankovskaya Street.

The men ran after him with a clatter of boots, and soon we heard them yelling: "Hold up there! Sto-p-p-p!"

We were used to hearing shouts like that in the night.

After about five minutes, my mother said, "You can come out now."

The ragamuffin burglar came crawling out of the laundry basket in the hall. He should have gotten down on his knees to my mother and thanked her for saving his life.

Instead, he spit, smoothed down his hair and started cursing us again.

My mother only looked at him with pity and hurried into the dining room, where the broken, trampled flowers were still lying on the floor among the crockery. The thief followed her quick movements as she put things to rights.

"What's your name?" she asked him, after sweeping the dirty floor clean.

The thief was silent for a few seconds, then said sullenly, "Top Hat."

My mother showed no surprise at such a peculiar name.

"Well then, Top Hat, I have some cherry dumplings left over from supper."

The thief threw himself on Mama's food and ate like a wild young animal. After that episode we had a saying in our family for people who gulped down their food without chewing it: "Why are you eating like Top Hat?"

After filling his belly he wanted to get out right away, but my mother made him stay there in the hall on the basket because she was afraid he might be picked up by the police at the gates. He left in the morning, and it was a long time before we saw him again.

About three months later I caught scarlet fever. It was a bad case. Dr. Kopp used to visit me every day and took two rubles for every three visits—big money! Even more was spent on the medicines and on the two medical consultations.

By winter we were down to nothing. Mama's ivory brooch and her gold bracelet and the samovar and the copper pots and the round mother-of-pearl earrings and even Marusya's tarnished watch—all of it had floated off to the pawnshop. In exchange we received green and purple receipts, very pretty. They crackled pleasantly and were decorated with crests and designs. Eight beautiful receipts, which I would take to bed with me while I was convalescing and look at for hours on end.

And then one day, when Mama was standing at the pawnshop counter, holding our last luxury item in her hands—a little box made of Karelian birch—she suddenly noticed Top Hat standing in the line. He laughed, "Ha-ha!" And he gave her a sly wink.

Under his arm was a sharp-nosed Turkish coffeepot of an odd shape, probably stolen last summer from some summer people.

"Gawd, what a dried-up old sea roach you are!" he said to her with a smile, as if he was handing her a compliment. "You're positively repulsive to look at!"

A sea roach is a kind of dried fish.

From my mother's haggard face, and from the almost worthless box she had brought to pawn, he realized that she was in trouble. She told him about my scarlet fever. He took her home, right up to the entrance gate, and that evening he came to visit us like an old friend. Without a word he made an expansive gesture and laid down in front of my mother a neat pile of ruble notes tied up with string.

"Put that away at once," said my mother, "or I'll call Simonenko."

Simonenko was the gray-haired, whiskered cop who lived in our house and practiced lugubriously on his trumpet every evening. At that very moment his trumpet was letting out hopeless, broken sounds.

Top Hat laughed.

My mother was furious and threw him out of the house. Soon he came back. And he kept coming back. Somehow, without our noticing how it happened, he came to be a member of our household. Marusya called him "Mama's thief."

He would arrive soundlessly in the dark with his catlike walk. Even the rusty iron plate that covered our garbage pit was silent under his feet. The pit was near our windows and everybody who came to visit us would step on that plate. The plate would bang against the cast-iron fence, and then a clanging would start up which made up for the fact that we didn't have a doorbell.

Only Top Hat knew how to step on the plate so that it didn't make the slightest sound. He would walk right through into our kitchen without saying hello to anybody, pick up the bucket from the stool and go to fetch water to fill our empty water barrel.

Since my mother was always busy over washtubs, doing people's laundry, she needed a lot of water; and there was no running water in our courtyard. She and Marusya and I had to fetch the water from a neighboring court in order to fill our thirsty water barrel, which sucked up all our strength. After we brought four bucketsful, things would turn green in front of our eyes, and our feet and hands would shake. And then we'd go for a fifth, a sixth and a seventh—or else Mama would have to go for the water herself, and we wanted to relieve her of that, Marusya and I.

But now Top Hat made himself our head barrel filler. It turned out that he was far from a "lazybones." Carrying our green bucket, he would race to the distant water faucet at a trot without stopping once to take a breath, and he wouldn't stop even when the barrel was full to the brim but would go on to fill the little tub in the entrance hall, the tin tub for boiling the wash that stood on the kitchen stove, the black bucket and even the pitcher for watering the plants.

Somehow, he entered right away into all our house-keeping concerns. When Mama sent him off to the market with me on a Sunday for herrings, tomatoes, eggplants, pears and "grain" (that is, ears of corn), he would bargain so hard over every kopeck that I would turn red out of shame in front of the peddlers.

Sunk in thoughts of Top Hat, my mother and my own misery, I didn't notice that I had arrived at home in our own courtyard. I didn't hear myself step on the sheet of iron that covered the garbage pit, although I usually tried to throw my whole weight on it to make it clang as loud as possible. Hunched over, on the point of tears, I walked up our three wooden steps and went into our one and only room, which my mother called "the living room."

# 6

## Mama and Uncle Foma

My mother was standing over the ironing board with her mouth full of water. Her cheeks were all puffed up, and from time to time she would form her lips into a "Pfrr! Pfrr! Pfrr!" sending the tiniest little sprinkles out of her mouth and onto the white shirt spread out in front of her. Then she would quickly pick up the heavy black iron from where it was standing on the tipped crown of the samovar and send it dancing along the shirt. It moved about merrily, as if it felt good being guided by such skilled hands.

My mother was a tall, dark-browed woman with a stately way of carrying herself. Her lovely face with its regular features was touched here and there with pock-marks, for she had been born into a peasant family where smallpox was a usual occurrence.

I never heard anybody call my mother a "washer-woman" and would have been quite surprised if I had.

And still, she washed other people's clothes that winter without taking time off to straighten her back; and the money she received for doing laundry was, I think, her only source of income.

She held herself very proudly and with great dignity. She didn't strike up friendships with any of the neighbors. On holidays, when she left our court, she would put on her lace-edged gloves and a black hat trimmed with glass beads. The bundles of dirty laundry would be delivered to her by Malanka, the daughter of a neighboring yard-keeper, who was also a little pockmarked. Malanka used to hang the wet laundry up to dry in the loft. Sometimes she stretched a clothesline between the barn and the two willow trees standing nearby in our courtyard, and hung the laundry outside, in front of our windows. Malanka addressed my mother as *Barynya*—"my lady." And the peddler who brought us pears, apples, vegetable marrows and cucumbers used to call my mother "Madam."

She did her washing only at night, in secret from us all. She would stand by the ironing board with her heavy iron for days on end. I couldn't picture that room without the ironing board even if I tried. The room wasn't big, but it was neat. The windows were covered with curtains, there were flowers, pillows and embroideries everywhere, and everything sparkled with cleanliness. My mother loved cleanliness with a passion, and threw herself into it with all her Ukrainian heart.

She would scrub the three ancient, unpainted wooden steps leading to our door with a scrubber and soap. Once I looked out of my window on a moonlight night and saw her out in the courtyard, washing the wooden boards laid out in a square in front of our porch. And the samovar!

And the candlesticks! And the brass mortar! Mama would polish them even when they were perfectly clean. She slept no more than two or three hours at night, and would gladly deny herself even that short rest if it suddenly entered her head to take some lime and whitewash the cellar.

How contemptuously she used to speak of Madam Shershenevich! "Gold earrings on her ears—and her neck's dirty!"

She could not forgive herself if a fluff of dust turned up under the couch or a spiderweb appeared behind the closet. She had a great deal of self-respect, never tried to get into anyone's good graces, never asked anyone for favors. And she walked majestically.

She talked in the way of southern Russia, with a kind of soft, singing lilt, half Ukrainian and half Russian. My sister Marusya was always correcting my mother's speech.

But I liked it when, instead of saying "neck" she'd say "nick," instead of "go get washed" she'd say "go git wished," instead of "dirty" she'd say "besmeared," instead of "sparrow" it would come out "sparling."

"Oh, Mama! You said 'sconion' again! It's 'onion,' not 'sconion'!" Marusya would try to teach her.

My mother was so shy about her lovely Ukrainian speech that she preferred to remain silent in front of strangers.

She was very trusting. Before buying a pear, an apple or some cherries from a passing peddler, she would ask him naïvely, "But are they good ones?"

"Very good ones, Madamochka, very good ones!" the peddler would answer without batting an eye, waving away the flies clustered over his basket.

"But isn't that rather expensive?"

"Oh no, Madamochka, it's not a bit expensive!"

And when the peddler would weigh out his produce Mama would ask him, "But are your scales accurate?"

"Oh yes, Madamochka, they're perfectly accurate!"

My mother was completely satisfied with answers like that, and was convinced that she had pulled off an excellent buy of first-class fruit, very cheap. But if, on the other hand, she saw that she was being swindled, she wouldn't say anything to the swindler—out of tactfulness.

At night, when she was scrubbing our cellar or whitewashing the kitchen, she would sing in time to her work, in a deep throaty voice, "Ai, on the Other Side of the Woods," or "Ekh, Underneath the Cherry Tree, Underneath the Cherry." I loved hearing those marvelous melodies through my sleep. But there were also times when she didn't sing. Or she would stop in mid-syllable if she became aware that someone was listening to her.

It was easy to make her laugh. When we read Gogol or Kvitka-Osnovyanenko she would fall into such a laughing fit, it was a strange sight. But I never saw her laughing with other people, or even exchanging smiles with a neighbor she passed in our court. She was very stern in her manner toward people, never paid visits on name days, never went to weddings or just out visiting. And when she was alone, an expression of deep sadness would form on her face.

But today of all days my mother was looking as happy as though she had never known any grief in her life. She looked at me in a young, enthusiastic way, barely able to hold herself back from blurting out some very pleasant piece of news.

"Wherever did you disappear to?" she asked me.

While I was on my way home I had decided that I would tell her the whole truth right away. I even had a little speech ready and planned to deliver it as soon as I crossed our doorstep. "Mama, please don't be scared. Everything is going to be just great, I promise you. Six-Eyes kicked me out of school."

But how could I dump such a heavy load on her that minute, when she looked so happy?

Better to tell her a little later . . . tonight . . . or tomorrow at teatime. Tomorrow. Tomorrow, at half-past seven. No point in upsetting her today.

This postponement was a terrific relief. That was how frivolous my character was. I cheered up right away and started asking all kinds of questions, as though nothing was wrong. What had happened today? And why was the cover off the couch?

She didn't answer me, only laughed and pointed her chin in the direction of the front hall. I dashed there and spotted a whip hanging on a hook.

How was it that I hadn't noticed it myself? I grabbed the whip, thrilled. (To this day I remember its slightly curved handle, worn smooth by the palm of its owner.) Beside myself with happiness, I shouted, "Uncle Foma's here! Uncle Foma's here!"

Only a tiny trace of unhappiness remained. All at once everything seemed beautiful—fabulous. I ran into the kitchen and cracked that magnificent whip, but Uncle Foma wasn't there. I searched for him under the bed and behind the barrels, certain that when I found him, my last drop of sadness would evaporate.

I ran to my mother and asked, "But where on earth is he?"

My mother smiled mysteriously and said he had gone to see somebody named Furnik, that he had been waiting for me, waiting a long time, and finally went by himself to this fellow Furnik, very far away, to Peresyp, and it wasn't at all certain whether he'd be coming back.

But I felt his pleasant smell all around me—pitch, honey, country bread and something else, something comfortable, special.

"He's here!" I shouted. "He's right here!"

And it was true. He was there, no more than two steps away. I opened the doors to the pantry wide. And there he stood, hardly breathing, hiding from me—a handsome, black-browed man in a coarse white canvas shirt. He looked at me without a hint of a smile on his face. My mother laughed till the tears ran down her face, she loved surprises so much. And I began to shout right away, "Popcorn! Popcorn!"

Whenever Uncle Foma came to visit us, he would bring grains of corn in a white canvas bag. Not just ordinary corn, but some kind of special corn that seemed like magic to us. We soaked it in water and then threw it into the oven, where it began to pop (you could hear it going "Pykh! Pykh! Pykh!"). It jumped around like some live thing. And we had to grab it the minute it started jumping around, so it wouldn't burn. And look! It had turned from yellow to white and was all puffed up like some wonderful bunch of flowers. I could have stood by the hot oven all day, throwing in more and more corn kernels and stuffing my belly with popcorn till I burst.

And yet all this seemed strange even to me. How was it that I—suffering under such a heavy load of sadness—could at the same time take so much pleasure in every pop and crackle of a corn kernel? Although I have to admit that my misery didn't really disappear. I felt it even when Uncle gave me the hedgehog and when I was running around the court in his sheepskin cap, jumping over the garbage pit like a savage, cracking his resounding whip.

"I have a hedgehog!" I shouted to the boys in the court. "Uncle Foma brought me a hedgehog!"

Burning with envy, the boys ran after me down the stairs to the cellar, and stared at the hedgehog with as much admiration as if he was a kangaroo or an elephant. I loved the hedgehog from the moment I became his owner. I fed him beets, cabbage and even little pieces of the brynza cheese Marusya gave me for dinner.

But when the boys went away and I was left alone in the cellar with my hedgehog, my eyes suddenly brimmed over with tears. If he only knew, my hedgehog, what a catastrophe I was postponing till tomorrow, and what was waiting for me in a few days, he would be my friend right away! He would cuddle up to me with all his prickles and purr.

But he wouldn't even look at me. He curled himself into a ball and snorted, and I couldn't even figure out where was his head and where were his feet.

Angrily, I shoved the last shreds of cabbage toward him and ran up the steps to Uncle Foma. Maybe he would recite for me the tale of the *shevchik*, the sly cobbler. I knew it by heart already, but I liked to listen to it over and over.

> *Cobbler sitting on a stool*
> *For his friends he plies his awl,*
> *Mending shoes with patches,*
> *Then the door begins to squeak,*

## Mama and Uncle Foma

*In the hut you hear a creak,*
*Bang! The door unlatches . . .*

But Uncle Foma was busy, sitting in the "living room" with my mother and ceremoniously drinking tea out of a glass. His relationship to my mother was amazing. He was her only brother, and she loved him with all her heart. But he was overawed by her and felt very stiff when he was sitting side by side with her. She would address him with the familiar "thee" and he would answer with the formal "you." She called him by his first name, Foma (his formal name was Foma Osipovich), but instead of calling her Katya he would address her formally as Katerina Osipovna.

When he was with her he felt ashamed of his country ways. She, a washerwoman, seemed like an important lady to him, and her humble apartment was a mansion in his eyes. He couldn't forget that he was in the city, where people talked differently and walked differently from country people. Drinking tea from a glass was an ordeal for him. The fork placed alongside the plate of sausage and dried fish scared him so much that he wouldn't eat.

And I couldn't forget that he was a countryman. I had never been to the country, and therefore a "countryman" seemed to me something like a redskinned Indian or a pirate or a sea captain. I lay there on top of the ironing board and waited. I knew that when the tea-drinking ordeal was over with, Uncle Foma would grab his country cap and run out to the barn to his country horse, and I would run after him. There, in the barn, the amusements and the wonders would start up. A little bottle would turn up from somewhere, and Uncle Foma would suddenly be transformed into a comedian and a wisecracker. All the draymen would gather around him and guffaw like mad at every word he said, because, as I now realize, he was a natural comic.

He could do an imitation of anybody he saw: our land-lord Spiridon Makry, and the old man Isak Mordukhai who owned the bar at the corner, and Madam Shershene-vich, and me, and Marusya, and Malanka, and even his own wife Ganna Dmitrievna. He would do a takeoff of her being scared by the thunder, and how when she saw a flash of lightning she would crawl inside the trunk. Opening his eyes wide and puffing his cheeks out, making himself somehow mysteriously smaller, my Uncle Foma would stick his thumb in his mouth.

With each new imitation he became a different person. Down to the last hair on his head he was changed into the gray-headed, whiskered cop Simonenko, trying to play the trumpet.

The draymen kept asking for more.

"And now Abrashka! Abrashka!"

"Do Motya! Motya!"

Motya was the draymen's cook. She was a giant of a woman with hair on her upper lip as thick as a moustache. She was forever cursing in her deep, rumbling voice. Uncle Foma not only imitated Motya—he actually be-came Motya. There she was to the life, standing by her stove burner, looking around furtively. She pulled a fiery hot piece of lard out of a huge kettle and hid it in her enormous bosom.

And even though Uncle Foma was actually holding nothing at all in his hand, you could almost see that soft, cooked, smoking hot piece of lard with the cloud of white steam rising out of it, you could see how it burned her hands and her chest, and how she threw it back into the kettle.

The audience would grow weak from laughing. They weren't guffawing any more—they were groaning. More and more people would come into the barn.

But just let my mother show herself at the door, and Uncle Foma would fall silent and even cover up his face with his cap. And then he'd go off deep inside the barn and start fussing around with some wheel or coupling bolt. This was something that never failed to amaze me, because Mama would have been only too happy to laugh along with him.

But in her presence Uncle Foma grew bashful to the point of speechlessness. He sat on the couch now stiffly and ceremoniously, burning his mouth on the hot tea, not daring to touch the sausage. Mama tried to start up a conversation on every subject imaginable, but he answered only "yes" or "no."

I don't know how their conversation ended, because I fell fast asleep right there on the ironing board.

# 7

## I Go Back to School

---

The next morning I woke up at dawn. My first thought was to run to my mother with the speech I had prepared for her yesterday. "Mama, please don't be scared. Everything is going to be just great, I promise you. Six-Eyes kicked me out of school."

Then a daring idea came into my head: to pick up my schoolbag and go to school as if nothing had happened. If I got there early, ahead of everybody, and sat down quietly at my desk, Six-Eyes might not even notice me. He was, after all, nearsighted. And even if he did see me—who knows? He might take pity on me, wave that little hand of his and say, "Well, all right, you can stay this time, but just remember . . ."

Or maybe he had forgotten all about yesterday? With so many really big things on his mind, after all! Perhaps in the heat of anger he had made a threat and then forgotten all about it. Yes—forgotten! Wasn't he always telling us his brains were scrambled on account of us? Why would he bother his head over such a trifle?

I wanted to believe this so much that I soon began to feel that nothing had happened yesterday. I got dressed, grabbed my cap and ran out into the still empty street, buckling my schoolbag around my shoulders as I went.

The clockmaker's window on Kanatnaya Street showed a quarter to seven. The air smelled of dust and spring rain. No one would be at school yet. I would get there long before classes started and sit down quietly to study my geography lesson. It would be very good to get a 5 in geography. History, too. Standing there at the intersection of Kanatnaya and Rybnaya, I made myself a promise that from this day on, if only they would keep me in the gymnasium, I would study like mad and get to be the top student in all subjects, outstripping even Adrian Sanda-gursky, who was number one in the whole school.

To my right, in back of St. Andrew's Church, stood the white building of the Kroll Gymnasium for Girls, set in its square of park and flooded with the bright pink rays of the morning sun. Rita Vadzinskaya, Lida Kuryndina and Timosha's sister Liza were students there. I looked at the path, striped with the long shadows of the trees, and wished hard for Rita to appear there. I even thought I saw her walking under the trees, but no, it wasn't Rita.

I had been in love with her for the past year. If I so much as caught a glimpse of her from a distance, something cool like the taste of peppermint would come into my chest. My feet would slow down as if they were walking a tightrope strung out over the tops of the houses. No power on earth could make me look her in the face. Even at a distance, my neck would stiffen into iron, and I could have sunk through the earth in embarrassment.

How strange it seemed to me that nobody else was the least bit shy with her, and that everybody talked to her as if she was a perfectly ordinary girl! And how strange that her father owned a pharmacy where anybody could walk in at any time and buy a corn plaster. His corn-plaster ads were pasted up all over the walls of our city.

We boys were not allowed inside the Kroll Gymnasium. We were strictly forbidden even to loiter in the vicinity. But in spite of this, the three of us—Munya, Timosha and I—had figured out a way of saving the girls from any crisis that might come up during a lesson. No matter that the girls sat locked inside their classroom walls, two blocks away from the boys' school. We organized a post office so reliable that the real postal service might well envy it.

Two of our teachers, Ivan Mitrofanych and Father Melety, served as the innocent postmen. The postal boxes were their galoshes.

Ivan Mitrofanych and Father Melety taught at both schools—ours and the Kroll Gymnasium. Every day at a set time they traveled the two blocks from the girls' school to the boys'. After a couple of hours, they would go back to the girls' school again. They would take off their coats and hats in the general cloakroom and leave their galoshes there before going into the teachers' room.

As soon as they left, we would steal into the cloakroom and plunge our hands inside the galoshes. If we found a message from the girls, we would have an answer ready before the hour was up, and deposit it back inside the same galosh. The unsuspecting teacher, plodding through the slush in those galoshes, would then carry our message into the Kroll Gymnasium, where one of the girls would be waiting for it.

But now it was spring. The Odessa streets were dried up, and nobody went around in galoshes any more.


I reached the gymnasium. There was the heavy oak door. Nobody here yet. I entered the vestibule, sat down at my desk and pulled my textbooks out of my school-bag. *Geography*, by Georgy Yanchin. The rivers of Siberia. I opened my atlas and began going over the names.

The Lyena. The Ob. The Yenisei. The Kolyma. The Angara . . .

Inside of fifteen minutes I knew the name of every single river in Siberia by heart, backward and forward, in every possible order. Fantastic rivers, swollen with streams, fertile with fish! How those names rang out: Khatanga, Indigirka, Anadyr!

The floor polishers arrived, gliding along with no expression on their faces, and wiping the hall floors. Up to now I hadn't particularly liked the smell of floor wax, but today I breathed it in with pleasure because it was the smell of school.

Galikin, our drawing teacher, whom we called "Fido," floated into the teachers' room to tidy up his droopy side-whiskers with a broken comb. He was the supervisor of the older classes, a wrinkled, angry old man with a hoarse voice and vacant eyes. He not only looked like an old mongrel dog, he even coughed like one.

But today he was dear to me. Not exactly dear, maybe, but pitiful. They said he had a disease called catarrh. His thin sidewhiskers drooped sadly this morning. Poor shabby old Fido! It couldn't be easy for him, being angry all the time.

Our geography teacher, Vasily Nikitich Volkov, walked in. He was an odd but good-natured old bird—the one for whom I had memorized the names of the rivers of Siberia this morning.

But where was my friend and ally—our history teacher Ivan Mitrofanych, or "Finti-Monti," as we called him? It would be good to see that strong, stubborn face of his. Finti-Monti was a man with peculiarities of his own. Whenever he got angry, he would fire a whole barrage of names at us, always in the same sequence. "Blockheads! Penny-whistlers! Loudmouths! Finti-Montis! Beetles on the fence!" All these weird names would fly out of his mouth in one breath, and he never changed the order.

If you seemed not to know the lesson, he would call you over, as if to congratulate you and pat you on the head. "Come over here . . . closer . . . closer . . ." he would say. When you came up and stood at the edge of the lectern he would smile and say, "Now just pick up that pen, dip it in the inkwell and mark down in this little space here— no, not there, right here—a zero."

Giving yourself a zero—that was like slapping your own face. You would write a tiny zero, hardly visible.

"But why such a skinny one? Make it fatter. Don't be bashful."

Why he did this I don't know. But we had grown accustomed to this peculiarity of his; and since zeros were a rarity for Ivan Mitrofanych and he handed them out only when they were earned in full, this procedure had long ago stopped causing hard feelings.

And, on the other hand, he taught us in a very special

way. I couldn't believe that I would be expelled from school and never again hear his husky monotone reciting the story of how the Tartar yoke was overthrown, and telling about Ivan the Terrible and the Time of Troubles, of false pretenders to the throne, of Vladimir Monomakh and Kuzma Minin. It was from Finti-Monti that we first heard certain names which were never mentioned in our textbooks of Russian history, names like Alexander Radishchev, Konrad Ryleyev, Alexander and Mikhail Bestuzhev and Alexander Herzen.* Everything he told us was so fascinating that even the Babenchikov brothers listened with their mouths open.

Here the Babenchikovs were, coming in now. They walked to their desks, noisily sucking on chocolate candy and wiping their chocolate spit with their sleeves. Why were these blabbermouths and loafers, who took no interest in anything but dirty stories and cards (I'd bet they had a pack of worn-out playing cards in their schoolbags that minute)—why were these birdbrains rewarded with 4's, promoted from grade to grade, to become college students with green uniforms in four years, while I . . .

But what was I complaining about? Here I was, still sitting at my own desk, the same as I had sat yesterday and a week ago. Nobody was kicking me out, everything was fine, and all around me were my schoolmates, with whom I had spent five years under one roof.

Zuyev came in, shuffling his feet like an old man, his heavy head bent low on his chest. He even smelled like

---

* Radical writers and critics. Radishchev was imprisoned by Catherine the Great; Ryleyev was hanged for his part in the Decembrist Uprising; Herzen spent years in exile in England.

an old man, a mixture of coffee, church incense, vinegar, cats and medicine, perhaps valerian drops. He would make the sign of the cross over his inkwell, his notebooks and his penholder with quick little movements. Then he would look up at the icon of the bald and bearded prophet Nathan hanging on the wall, cross himself and recite in his old man's way:

> *Nathan, holy prophet,*
> *Give my brain your profit!*

I knew Zuyev by heart. I even knew that since today was Saturday he had been out on the street early, running to all the churches and chapels to pray that our teachers would catch the cholera and drop dead.

Our financial wizard came in—Aristides Okudzhalla. For two years now he had been running a profitable business venture in class. He insured us against bad marks. We would go to Okudzhalla before some specially threatening lesson—written algebra, say, or oral Latin—and deposit five kopecks in his treasury. If we got a passing grade our money stayed in the treasury. If it was 1 or 2, Okudzhalla instantly lightened the pain by handing over five or six five-kopeck coins. If we weren't called on at all, the money was lost.

To his credit, Okudzhalla kept only a small percentage for himself. In general he ran his business honestly and didn't try for big profits. His firm was flourishing.

But if I managed to stay on here at the gymnasium, Okudzhalla would never get another kopeck out of me. I'd work like a dog and be the top student in our class.

And here came poor miserable Kozelsky with his eyes

all red from crying. Today and tomorrow he would have to stay after school in the detention room for four hours "for forging marks and concealing his report card." Lucky for him that his father was away in Tiraspol. He was spared parental correction with bare fists, so what was the blockhead crying about? I would have been glad to sit in our detention room for twenty hours—for two hundred hours—if only Six-Eyes would let me stay here on this bench.

Munya Blokhin arrived, all in a sweat and out of breath. He must have run the whole way from where he lived on Moldavanka so as not to be late. Today it was his turn to be class monitor.

"Hello, Munya!"

"Pfah! You here?" He looked at me in amazement and sat down on the edge of my bench. "But I heard that you . . . they . . ." He made a gesture with his fist to signify someone getting shoved out the door.

"It's the truth, Munya. They really did kick me out," I said.

I tried to smile; but the moment I put my misery into words, I realized the hopelessness of my situation for the first time.

I felt so sorry for myself, my chin started shaking. I could feel a few tears splashing down on Yanchin's *Geography*, irrigating the already swollen waters of the rivers of Siberia.

"They did kick me out . . . but just the same I came . . . because . . ."

He nodded his head understandingly.

"I came here and I'm staying here . . . like always . . . I thought, maybe they won't even notice I'm here. Maybe they'll forget the whole thing . . . I came, and I'm staying . . . because . . ." I tried to cry without making any noise, but I got the hiccups and started to choke.

Munya smacked his lips doubtfully. "You think they might not notice? Oy-oy! Well, maybe you're right—how do we know? Let's give it a try. But you'd better sit over here. You sit in my place and I'll sit in yours. I'll stick out my elbows and make a screen for you."

This was piddling help, but he wasn't in a position to offer me anything better, so I took his advice.

# 8

## Behind Munya's Back

As luck would have it, nobody took any interest in me even though it was now nine twenty-seven, when the supervision was particularly strict. This was the time when Six-Eyes would fly down the corridor looking into each room in turn and saying the same thing to each class: "Cease—this—hideous—racket—im-med-i-ate-ly." And then he would continue on his rounds, tiptoeing in that strange, prissy walk of his.

It was also the time when Prokhor Evgenych, our inspector, patroled the halls. He too would stick his head inside every door and say "Sh-h-h!" Prokhor Evgenych—or, as we called him, Proshka—used to trail the students on soft-soled shoes. He was always watching us out of the corner of his eye, sneaking up on us, listening in. He was an intriguer and a spy, and we all hated him. If we were out on the street after seven in the evening, if our schoolbags weren't properly buckled around our shoulders by both clasps, if we failed to notice him and tip our hats to him when we were walking around a puddle, he would write down our names in his little notebook. The next day, we'd be sitting in the detention room after school.

The bell rang. Our French teacher, Monsieur Lan, flitted into our room, mopping his brow with the tip of his scarf. There was nothing frightening about Monsieur Lan. Although he had immigrated to Russia long ago, he still didn't understand the Russian language.

Monsieur Lan was like a man who had fallen from the moon. He didn't recognize a single student by sight and couldn't keep straight which of his classes he was in. In several years of teaching, he hadn't managed to teach us one word of French. No, that wasn't fair—we did learn one French word. We learned that *l'âne* meant "jackass."

Today, again, I fell to wondering why he had such a peculiar name. Whether he really was a jackass I couldn't say, because I had never spoken to him. Seven or eight lucky boys in our class had known French practically from their cradles, and Monsieur Lan used to chatter away with them, laugh with them, and raise his finger before making a witty remark. The rest of us got no attention from him. I often thought that if the blacksmith Vaska Pechonkin had been put behind my desk instead of me, Monsieur Lan wouldn't have noticed.

But just the same, there was something rather pleasant about him. Today, I could see that. Even his famous scarf failed to produce its usual sneer from me. What was so awful about that scarf, after all? Monsieur Lan used it not only to wrap his neck in, but also to polish his shoes, to wipe chalk from the blackboard and to blow his nose.

If I stay on at the gymnasium, I told myself, I'll learn

French inside of two or three months. Not without envy, I watched Lan conversing with Sandagursky, Saburov and the other "aristocrats" in our class. And anyway, I thought, a scarf can be washed.

The bell rang again. The boys ran out into the hall for recess. But I just went on sitting there, trying to look as inconspicuous as possible. Since the monitor for the day was Munya, nobody bothered me.

Munya opened the little transom window and then ran to the office for a bottle of ink, but came back right away.

"They're coming! Six-Eyes and Proshka!"

I started running around the room. Where could I hide? Behind the stove? Under the lectern?

But it turned out that there was nothing to get into a panic about. Six-Eyes and Proshka stalked right past our room and went next door to the sixth-year class, where, as we found out later, there had been a minor event. Someone had put a cat into the chalk box under the blackboard. That was why the two of them were sneaking up on the scene of the crime. Together with Fido, Vasily Afanasievich and Pyzhikov (the supervisor of the younger boys, whose classrooms were located on the floor below) they proceeded to administer justice.

So that meant I had nothing to worry about for at least another half hour or maybe even an hour.

The next lesson, geometry, also went satisfactorily. And since the case of the cat was still going on next door I used my reprieve to the full. During the second recess I ran out into the hall and dashed down its whole length, from the wall where the clock was hanging to the wall with the icons on it. (This wall was separated from the hall by a wooden gate, behind which Six-Eyes had set up a small

chapel, as if made to order for Zuyev, who stopped there
to cross himself even on his way to the toilet.)

I raced back and forth, skating along the waxed floor
although, along with the others, I kept glancing through
the glass doors of the sixth-year classroom as I passed. The
students inside were still standing at attention while Six-
Eyes cut them up with the wooden saw of his harangue.

The bell rang. As I got back to my desk, my friend
Timosha beamed at me. He must have been worried all
this time, not knowing what was going on with me. I sat
down at my place and opened up my textbook in Russian history: reign of Catherine II, paragraphs 8 and 9.
Now Ivan Mitrofanych would come in, and we'd hear
that barrage of friendly abuse again: "Blockheads!
Penny-whistlers! Loudmouths! Finti-Montis! Beetles on
the fence!"

But it wasn't Ivan Mitrofanych who walked in, it was
Six-Eyes; and behind him a tall, powerfully built man
with a carefully groomed beard.

Six-Eyes arranged his pince-nez on top of his spectacles,
stepped forward and made an announcement. "I am here
to introduce you to your new teacher, Igor Leonidovich
Gudima-Karchevsky, and to tell you how grateful you
should be to Divine Providence for having sent you such
a mentor. The ancient Russian sources of monarchi-
cal power . . ."

More phrases like that followed, boring and meaning-
less to us. But it could only mean one thing: the new
teacher was a replacement for Ivan Mitrofanych.

Six-Eyes went away. The new teacher crossed himself
three times before the icon of the prophet Nathan, then

raised his powerful shoulders. With a heavy, assured step he began walking between the rows of desks.

He turned to Tuntin. "What is your assignment?"

"Catherine the Second, paragraphs eight and nine."

"Not true. Out of your seat! Arms at your sides, stand up straight like a pillar. . . . Now then—you!"

"Our assignment is Catherine the Great, paragraphs eight and nine."

"Not true. Stand up like a pillar. All right—you!"

No matter whom he questioned, he got the same answer. And he made each one stand up. When more than a dozen "pillars" were collected, he looked them over disgustedly, then began to talk in a tired, wounded voice.

"Not 'Catherine,' but the *Em-press Catherine the Great*. Any servant girl can be called Catherine. But her Im-*per*-i-al *High*-ness Catherine the Great, who rectified our morals, laid the foundations of our science, gladdened our fatherland with the conquest of new territories . . ."

He looked ready to burst into tears any minute.

"And may I give you this general warning," he contined. "Any one of you who, during a history lesson, should refer to any of the *Auto*-crat *Em*-per-ors as simply Paul, or simply Alexander, or Nicholas, or Ivan, will receive from me . . ." here his face glowed like the sun ". . . a . . . *zero*."

The bell rang for the long recess, but he went on talking.

Munya turned to me and whispered, "What the heck is going on here . . . to fire Finti-Monti for such a nitwit."

"You don't mean to say they fired Finti-Monti?" I asked.

"Pfah! They fired him a week ago. On Saturday."

"How do you know?"

Munya roomed in the apartment of our geography teacher and therefore he got to know a lot of school secrets.

But who had fired Finti-Monti, and why? What had he done? He was our friend and ally. There was no other teacher in the school that we students liked better than Finti-Monti.

Once, at the end of our third year when we were ready for promotion, the head of all the churches unexpectedly came to visit our school to be present at our final exam in religious instruction. It was the Right Reverend Bishop Diomedes. He was greeted at the stairs with a special hymn of welcome. Six-Eyes and the other teachers crowded around the entrance to kiss his hand; and we students sat in our classroom cold with fear—for we couldn't expect leniency from our examiners in the presence of such an important personage.

At that time, religious instruction was considered the most important and difficult subject. We had to know dozens of prayers and Gospel texts by heart. It would have been disastrous to flunk that exam.

But lo and behold—while Six-Eyes and his retinue were fussing around in the entrance hall, Finti-Monti walked into our class, and inside of a few minutes we were all rescued from the catastrophe which threatened us. Without saying a word Finti-Monti approached the examination table, picked up six or seven "tickets" from its very edge (each ticket had an exam question written on it, which we would have to answer), and then began holding up these questions and showing them to our startled class. He did this slowly enough for us to make a mental note of the order in which they were placed on the desk. Then he went through the same procedure with the rest of the tickets. By the time the Bishop, supported on both sides by Father Melety, Six-Eyes, Fido and Proshka, was installed behind the examination table, every student knew where the questions were located on the table. I, for example, had memorized question no. 24. Having noted that that particular ticket lay to the right of the inkwell, I stretched out my hand to it when my turn came, and recited my answer without hemming or hawing. The Bishop nodded his head benignly and gave me a nice big fat 5.

The rest of my classmates, almost to a man, received 5's also. And it was all thanks to the help of Finti-Monti, who, as I found out later, was a violent opponent of clericalism. And besides that, we sensed with some deep instinct that he disliked Six-Eyes and all his "archangels" (as he called them) just as much as we did—and that they felt the same way about him.

At last our new teacher Gudima-Karchevsky turned to the door. Immediately the students, roaring and stamping, whistling and pushing, piled out after him into the hall.

I ran out with them, trying to keep myself in the thick of the crowd so as not to be seen by Proshka or Six-Eyes. If only recess was over with! After that, there was nothing more to worry about. The first class after recess was Latin. My classmates hated it, but I took to it from the very first lesson and enjoyed it still. Words in Latin seemed like treasures to me—resonant, noble, simple, proud, beautiful! I knew that if our Latin teacher Kavun called me to the blackboard, he would nod after every answer and say "*Bene.*" There was nothing to fear from Kavun.

And after Latin, geography. Nothing to worry about

there either. The rivers of Siberia—Khatanga, Angara, Indigirka and so forth.

And then—home! To my own house on Rybnaya Street. Where Uncle Foma was visiting from the country. And a hedgehog was waiting for me in the cellar, and tomorrow was Sunday, and Timosha would come to see me. Timosha, my best friend.

# 9

# Not Through the Front Door and Not Through the Back Door

Timosha and I had been friends almost from the first day he came to school, when we were nine and in the first-year class. Flames started shooting out of the stove in the hallway outside our room, and someone yelled "Fire!" Timosha got scared and confessed later, with a stammer, "Ev-v-ven m-m-my heart w-was p-p-palpitating."

To tell the truth he didn't even say "palpitating" but "pulpitating."

Lots of the boys started to laugh at him because "pulpitating" sounded so funny. Timosha had only just come to Odessa from Arkhangelsk, and his north Russian speech sounded weird to us.

Nobody liked him then. He was freckle-faced and he had big ears. On top of that, he stuttered. When he stuttered he sprayed spit, so everybody would run away without listening to him. He loved to talk. In those early days I was the only one who was willing to listen.

At first I did this only because I felt sorry for him. But soon something very odd happened. While he was talking to me, Timosha's stutter almost disappeared. With other people, he stuttered just as much as before, but when the two of us were alone his speech was as smooth and easy as any other boy's. And in his fascinating north Russian dialect, which he had brought with him from the White Sea to the Black, he used to tell me all kinds of exciting tales—about Sinbad the sailor and his adventures with the giant bird Roc, Aladdin and his magic lamp, enchanted caves filled with golden vessels, underground gardens swarming with monsters.

But Timosha's best stories were about smugglers and pirates whom he had supposedly seen with his own eyes. His father was a Customs official who used to capture smugglers by the dozen. Or so Timosha said.

Later I came to realize that all these stores about smugglers were no more than Timosha's fantasies. But at the time I believed every word, and I was terrifically excited by them. These smugglers were all daredevils, giants who held long pistols in their gleaming white teeth. But Timosha's father was braver and more daring than all of them put together. He would ride out into the storm, in the Customs cutter, alone against the whole band. Laughing at their pistol fire, he would capture them as easily as Gulliver captured the Lilliputians.

The first time I met Timosha's father face to face, I was flabbergasted. This menacing pirate killer was only an ordinary office clerk. His skin was the color of clay and he was getting bald. He went around in felt boots even in summertime because of his rheumatism. It's possible that Timosha had invented for himself a different father for the very reason that his real father was sickly and boring.

It was in the back court of my house that Timosha used to talk about the exploits of this invented father. That was where the kalamashki stood—those unpainted half-round boxes like tremendous deep troughs, where the snow and accumulated rubbish used to collect. During our free time Timosha and I loved to climb inside a kalamashka, lie down in its splintery, crooked bottom and whisper all kinds of tall stories to each other. For some reason we called this "talking about Bagdad."

Later, when we were in the third-year class and followed the weekly installments of an adventure magazine Timosha's mother subscribed to, *Around the World*, we would still climb into that same kalamashka to tell each other stories about cannibals and cowboys, pathfinders, volcanoes and African mirages. It was a very peculiar thing. The minute we got settled down in the bottom of our kalamashka, rocking as if we were inside a boat and "talking about Bagdad," we felt transported to another country. And we ourselves became different people than we had been a minute ago, when we were teasing Filimon the goat or getting into a fight with Vaska Pechonkin's street gang.

It was there inside our kalamashka, when we were thirteen and in the fifth-year class, that I told Timosha two important secrets which I had never told a living soul—one, that I was in love with Rita Vadzinskaya, and two, that I wrote poetry. I talked about this only inside the kalamashka. The minute we climbed out such conversations stopped. Timosha would have been amazed if, in school or out on the street, I ever mentioned a word of what we used to talk about inside the kalamashka.

And now Timosha ran up to me, excited and happy. "Hey, look how great it all came out! Now there's nothing to worry about. I bet even Six-Eyes is sorry he lit into you like he did."

He gave me a clap on the shoulder. A heavy weight seemed to roll off my chest. It was true! The danger was over. All my troubles evaporated. I felt a terrific hunger. Or rather, it wasn't until now that I noticed that I hadn't eaten anything all day, since I had run out of the house at the crack of dawn, without food or money.

Just then a crowd of students began storming the table in the corridor where Pushkin the food seller had covered a stained tablecloth with food—sausage, ham, bread-and-butter sandwiches. I asked Pushkin to let me have a French roll or a sesame seed roll on credit.

He looked at me suspiciously, then took a stale, wrinkled roll out of a basket and shoved it at me sourly. Oy— such a little one! I could have eaten five or six like that.

"Pushkin, can't I please have one more?"

A voice rang out from behind my back. "Per-mit me! Just a minute there!"

I turned around. It was Proshka, the school inspector. Yellowish whiskers like a cockroach. And a satisfied look on his face.

"Just what do you think you are doing here, esteemed sir?"

I looked at him. For some reason I showed him my French roll. "Here—I bought it—I mean, I didn't exactly buy it, but—I mean, I'll pay for it tomorrow—but today . . ."

"This institution is not your bakery, esteemed sir!" he

said. "Or didn't you notice our sign on the front door—
Students Only. No Admittance to Outsiders!"

The students standing around fell into a hushed silence.
There must have been a hundred, and more kept coming.

"This institution is not your bakery!" he repeated, looking not at me but at the crowd. He looked like an actor
who had finally won the part he was after, and was now
prepared to play it to the hilt.

"Prokhor Evgenych!" I began incoherently. "I didn't
mean—it wasn't my fault—ask Kozelsky—ask Zuzya.
Zuzya, why don't you speak up? You know I never saw
your report card. Honest to God I never saw it, Prokhor
Evgenych! All my friends will tell you! There's Tuntin—
ask Tuntin."

"No, my dear sir! Pardon me! *There* are your friends—
out there!" And he pointed out the window, where a
crowd of ragged, homeless children were standing around
by the iron gates of the monastery park. In our town they
were called "the barefoots."

"Wouldn't you care to invite those gentlemen over
here?" Proshka sneered. "Take seats at the desks, my
dears, and we'll teach you algebra, chemistry and all the
languages."

This was Proshka's favorite topic. For many years he
had been saying that gymnasiums exist only for a select
few. Today he developed this subject at length. And only
now did I notice that Six-Eyes was also there, standing
near the "sobbing room." With a frown on his face, he
was nodding "yes" to every word Proshka said.

Proshka was Six-Eyes' ape. He imitated all his movements, he made the same kind of flowery speeches. He

even had a nearsighted squint like Six-Eyes, although his vision was perfect.

I heard him through a fog. Timosha, all upset and white in the face, was standing opposite me, with a look of burning hatred for Proshka in his eyes. He was so angry, his cheeks were shaking and his lips kept moving. He was straining to say something, but couldn't get a word out because of his stutter. The slightest emotional upset made him lose his tongue. All he could do was make a mooing noise.

And Ludwig Meier, a senior classman, was standing there too.

Proshka turned to me with exaggerated politeness. "Be good enough, my dear sir, to take yourself off!" Then he said to the young porter's helper Kostya in a different voice, "Look how the foxy-loxy tries to sneak in here! 'I have come, Prokhor Evgenych, for a roll!' he says."

Now Tuntin put in his piece. "And he's been here all morning."

"All morning, is it? Oho! Now then, Kostya, pay attention to what I'm telling you. If this *signor* ever shows his face here again, he is not to be admitted. Not through the front door and not through the back door. Don't even let him inside the vestibule. And now, young man, *if* you please . . ."

"Prokhor Evgenych!" It was Munya from a distance, trying to squeeze through the crowd. "Prokhor Evgenych! You don't understand, I'll explain it to you!"

Prokhor stared at Munya with that ominous expression Six-Eyes used on his worst "sobbers" and didn't bother to answer. Turning to me again, he said, "Pick up your things, young man, if you have any. If you will be good enough to follow me . . . right this way, my dear sir!"

He kept pointing out the way, as if I had never been inside the school before. "To the right, sir . . . to the left, sir." Walking in front of me and with Kostya in back, he led me to the exit the way a policeman leads a prisoner.

"Wait a minute—*please!*" It was Munya again, held back by the crowd of first-year kids piling up in the lower corridors.

I kept on walking with my eyes looking down. I felt ashamed, in the midst of my own schoolmates, like a thief caught with the goods.

Munya managed to squeeze through.

"Prokhor Evgenych, it was only for two weeks that they suspended him . . . just till the School Board meets. I heard it myself—they told me—I guess you don't know . . ."

"The School Board met already. Last night. A special meeting. They voted to expel him for good. Him and two more besides."

When I heard those terrible words I didn't fall down on the floor. I didn't start howling and I didn't burst into tears. There just wasn't room inside of me to hold any more misery.

Timosha was telling me something. I couldn't understand it, I couldn't hear it. I felt as if I was deaf and dumb.

We started going down the stairs to the cloakroom. Here I knew every step, every spot on the wall by heart. The first-year kids, the nine-year-olds, were standing around in the vestibule, staring at me. They probably thought I was a gangster who would do them harm if I broke loose.

I kept walking down the steps.

I saw Father Melety inside the cloakroom. He was standing in front of the mirror and smoothing down his eyebrows with a little brush. From old habit I bowed to his reflection in the mirror. He looked right through me as if I was a fence or a tree.

Proshka shouted to the porter Moiseyich, "Hand the young man his cap!"

Students were never given their caps by the porter. I wanted to step over to my own hook, my own familiar coat hook, number 11, first on the left. But Proshka kept a tight hold on my shoulder.

"Kindly don't trouble yourself. It will be given to you immediately."

Grabbing my cap, he did a terrible thing. He ripped off the silver school crest. In total desperation I put on my dishonored cap and ran outside on the street, while my lips, of their own accord, senselessly went on repeating the words Khatanga, Angara, Indigirka, Lyena, Kolyma, Anadyr.

# 10

## A Battle and a Victory

The crest on my school cap, two oak leaves with two letters and a number between them—the name of our gymnasium—was made of a white plated metal which we called "silver." The crest cost thirty kopecks. My mother was prepared to give up several years of her life to keep it shining on my cap.

My mother knew that a boy with a silver crest on his cap could become an important lawyer or doctor or a famous professor. But a boy who didn't have those white oak leaves on his cap might at any time become a bum and disappear under the port bridge into the frozen night.

Of course it would be nice to become a sailor in the volunteer fleet, or a blacksmith like Vaska Pechonkin. But for that you had to have the strength of a Hercules. What mighty muscles Vaska had!

I went to his smithy on the corner of Kanatnaya and Bazarnaya and stood around for a while under his rusty sign with a big horseshoe and a little red two-legged horse painted on it. Vaska was naked to the waist, black with dirt and shiny with sweat. With one hand he was raising a hammer I wouldn't be able to lift with both of mine. He beat his hammer against a red-hot iron pig and twirled the pig around with his pincers like a walking stick, sending sparks flying into the air.

No. I was weak and clumsy. I wouldn't be much good as a blacksmith.

There was the Makry house, and there was our garbage pit, covered with its iron plate. My mother, thank goodness, wasn't at home. She had gone to the cemetery with Uncle Foma to visit the grave of my Aunt Elena, who died of cholera and whom I had never seen.

The cemetery was far away on the other side of the station, past Chumka. They wouldn't be back before 10 p.m., maybe even later. That meant she wouldn't find out about my misfortune today at all. I'd tell her the whole story tomorrow after Uncle Foma went home. Or better yet, the day after tomorrow—Monday morning. The day after tomorrow was far away. There were thirty-seven or thirty-eight hours ahead of me. All kinds of things could happen in thirty-eight hours.

I understood perfectly well that my relief was senseless and that there was nothing to hope for. I knew that the time would fly past like one minute. But just the same it was a pleasant feeling to be alone in the apartment with my sister Marusya.

A fit of gaiety took hold of me. I ran around the court-yard up to the gate and made my way along the ditch up to the loft where, surrounded by every variety of junk, I

had a little hideout of my own which I called "the Wigwam." Not a soul except Timosha knew about the Wigwam. The entrance to it was barricaded by empty barrels
labeled "Portland Cement," and you had to squeeze your
way into it as though into a narrow cave, under the very
ceiling.

It was very clean, cozy and quiet inside my Wigwam.
The floor was washed the way my mother would have
done it, with soap and a bast scrubber (it wasn't easy, getting a bucket of water in there). And the walls were
papered with pages from the magazine *Alarm Clock*,
which Simonenko the cop had given me as a present. The
floor was covered with armfuls of last year's hay cuttings,
still smelling of daisies, wormwood and mint. My military
weapons were hanging on the walls—a slingshot that
could shoot thirty paces and a semicircular, brightly
painted iron shield made by Uncle Foma.

Here in the Wigwam last summer I had written my
epic poem *Gymnasiada*, describing different events in our
school life. The poem was written in a three-kopeck school
notebook, and the notebook was shoved behind a ceiling
beam where no one could find it.

In order to reach the ceiling you had to stand on a
dilapidated, unsteady barrel. I scrambled up on it somehow and shoved another object behind the beam: my cap.
The cap with the crest torn off.

I felt better right away and hurried home again.

Marusya was sitting hunched over on the couch. Her
head was buried in a library book, *What the Swallow
Sang*. Marusya was reading it for probably the twelfth time.

"Take the cornmeal and fish out of the oven, and kindly

don't interfere with my reading," she said without taking her eyes from the page. Her voice was distinct and dry, as if she was reading dictation.

Marusya was stern, always working at something. She talked down to me from a height. She thought of me as a light-minded loafer. I was more afraid of her than of Mama. She was the top student in her class at the girls' gymnasium, and was already earning four rubles a month by giving lessons to Madam Shershenevich's niece. People praised Marusya because she was so serious, and found fault with me because I wasn't like Marusya. Mama was the only one who indulged me. Marusya was sensitive to this, and found it very wounding.

I would have loved to be serious like Marusya, but nothing concrete ever came out of this wish. Several times she had attempted to instruct me, but finally she gave up. Once, about three years ago, she said to me in an unexpectedly childlike voice, "Do you want to play travels?"

"Sure!" I answered.

I thought she meant ships crashing and sinking, stuff like that. But instead she took five little pieces of paper, wrote the words "Asia," "Africa," "Europe," "America" and "Australia" on them in a careful handwriting and then fastened them down with pins in different corners of our big courtyard. The draymen's kitchen turned out to be America, and Simonenko's porch was Europe. We took long sticks and traveled from Asia to America. As soon as we reached America Marusya frowned and said, "In America the chief rivers are such-and-such, the chief mountains are this-and-that, the chief countries are as follows, the climate is this, the plant growth is that."

And then she said, "Repeat that after me."

I didn't bother to answer. It would have been better if she had hit me! Traveling . . . for me, that meant dashing through the prairies, dying of yellow fever, digging up ancient treasures, rescuing beautiful Indian maidens from bloodthirsty sharks, killing cannibals and tigers with boomerangs. And here she was dragging me from one piece of paper to the next and trying to make me memorize dozens of names. Marusya loved games like that—useful games, educational games.

I ran away from her as soon as we reached Europe and hid out in the Wigwam all day. Ever since then Marusya had been convinced that I was a light-minded loafer, and she treated me like a nonentity.

After I finished my supper and washed the dishes she called me over and said, "If I were you I would go get some water, because both barrels are absolutely empty."

She loved the word "absolutely" and other bookish words that nobody else used, like "from the point of view of," "intellect," "individuum."

"Aye, aye, sir!" I said with a laugh. I was amazed at myself. Where did that laugh come from? As though nothing was wrong!

I picked up the green bucket and ran down the street. The water faucet was in the Petrokokino house, several courts away, where there were also bullocks, drays and draymen. A dray is a special kind of long, heavy cart. A pair of bullocks would be hitched up to a cart and early in the morning, before sunrise, two or three dozen carts would file toward the harbor to unload and load the steamships. Alongside the bullocks walked the draymen—sunburnt, powerful men in torn and faded shirts. All day

under the broiling sun they ran up and down the gang-
planks carrying 250-pound bags of currants, vanilla beans,
resin, coffee, paprika, figs, olives and almonds. The draymen were saturated through and through with the smells
of their goods, the smells of Turkey, Greece, Asia Minor,
Africa. They liked me (even though they used to call me
"Gawky") and often gave me a handful of sunflower seeds
or sweet cookies.

But there were no draymen there today. They were all
at the bathhouse, because it was Saturday. I went down
Rybnaya Street again, with my bucket full of water.

I stopped at the Wagner house to take a breath. I put
my bucket down on the wooden footway even though I
knew this was a dangerous thing to do. The Wagner house
was where the enemy lived. I could never bring myself to
go inside that house because I was convinced that they
would scratch out my eyes, tear out my tongue and cut off
my ears. In it lived a bunch of tough guys who had
been at war with our house as long as I could remember.

We called their gang "the Pechonkies" because the
blacksmith and tinsmith Vaska Pechonkin was their
leader. Whenever anybody from our house carried a
bucket of water past a Pechonky, the Pechonky would
try to spit in the bucket or throw something filthy into it.

We, the fellows who lived in the Makry house, were
known as "the Makrukies." We didn't let the Pechonkies
pass us either, and we tried to pull as many dirty tricks on
them as we could. Our landlord's youngest son had a
slingshot. He would bop the Pechonkies with it whenever
they passed us sticking their tongues out or making a
"fig" at us with their thumb in their fists.

I hated every one of them. If anybody had ever told me

then that they were human beings just like us, the guys from the Makry house, I wouldn't have believed it. I had a special hate for a fellow called Witaway. He was about fourteen and he had a funny-looking narrow head like a cucumber. And there he was, hiding behind a ledge in the wall near the gate, lying in wait for me.

I waited for some passerby to come along and protect me, but the street was empty. I crossed over to the other side, where the Army barracks was. An officer was looking at me out of the barracks window with about as much sympathy as an iron post. I ran with all my might. But the water was splashing out of the bucket, and I had to slow down. There was something in Witaway's fist—a round, black, dried-up ball of crap.

"O-pa-pa!" Witaway let out his redskin war cry and jumped across the street toward me.

I ran to the barracks gate. More water splashed out of my bucket. I put the bucket down by the wall. Witaway let out another "o-pa-pa," ran into me and butted me in the stomach with his head. I dashed over to the wall and watched while he spit into the bucket twice and threw the ball of crap into it. His spit was white and slimy, like a horse foaming at the mouth.

I let out a yell and tried to sink my nails into his cheeks. But he threw me back against the same wall and shouted his victory shout: "O-pa-pa!"

The Army officer went on watching us from behind the window.

All of a sudden a mighty ally came to my defense. He pranced out of the barracks and threw himself at the enemy like a train engine. It was Filimon, the Army goat and mascot, famous all up and down our street as a fighter and a drunkard. If people behaved themselves peaceably Filimon didn't bother them. But if anybody started a fight, Filimon would be transformed from a goat into a tiger. He would come at one of the fighters on the run and butt him from behind, in back of the knees (not with his horns but with the front of his head), so unexpectedly that the unlucky one would fall flat on his face.

Filimon got drunk only on holidays. He watched the draymen going past the barracks to the tavern and followed them, and you couldn't chase him away even with a stick. The draymen were glad to give him vodka to drink. Sometimes they soaked pieces of bread in vodka and fed him this alcoholic bread, which he would gobble up greedily. When he went home he would be wobbling from side to side and bumping into the poles and lampposts just like a drunken drayman. The boys from the neighboring houses would tease him, pull him around, grab him by the horns and push him, but he didn't defend himself. He was as mild and quiet as a lamb. He would stagger into the barracks, sprawl down in the stable at the feet of Cheremis, the regimental horse, and fall asleep.

Luckily Filimon was sober today. Witaway was not going to escape the blows of his powerful goat forehead. Witaway fell flat on the footway while the goat stood over him and shook his beard like Father Melety, laughing spitefully: "Me-h-h-h!"

Witaway tried to get up but Filimon got him behind the knees again, and again he was stretched out full length on the footway.

I was happy. I danced around like a savage and then I grabbed my bucket. Shouting "O-pa-pa!" I emptied its whole filthy contents on Witaway's head.

Witaway snorted, jerked his legs, spit out violently, then turned his wet, red, furious face toward me. Looking at the goat, he tried to get up. But I put the bucket right over his head and drummed on it with my fists. "O-pa-pa! O-pa-pa! O-pa-pa!"

Witaway started bawling so loud the whole street could hear him.

"What are you doing, you bastard! Leave the child alone!" It was Witaway's mother, yelling at me out of her window.

I just barely kept enough control over myself not to stick my tongue out at her. I picked up my bucket and ran. My victory filled me with triumph. I ought to be ashamed to mention this, but when I fell asleep on my folding cot that night before my mother came home, what I thought about was not the calamity that had happened to me that day, but only my victory over Witaway. And the way I was going to brag about this great victory to all the fellows in our house. And what we Makrukies were going to do tomorrow, Sunday, to defeat the Pechonkies in open warfare, and how we would take their leader Vaska Pechonkin a prisoner.

That was our oldest, fondest dream—to take revenge on the blacksmith for all his dirty tricks.

It was a funny thing. We hated him, but only on holidays. On weekdays we loved to stand at the door of his smithy at the corner of Kanatnaya and Bazarnaya Street and follow every movement of his soot-stained hands with respectful curiosity, watch him shoe a horse or force a tire on a wheel. At times like that we even liked him.

But on holidays he would wash off the soot, smear his hair with pomade, put on a lemon-yellow shirt and throw a sky-blue jacket over his broad shoulders, the kind of jacket they call a *tvinchik*. And then he would immediately become our enemy, a different person. His eyes would narrow into slits, he'd get a sly, crooked sneer on his face. He never even looked at us Makrukies, never talked to us and therefore seemed even more terrible to us. It was the Pechonkies who made up his loyal army.

The people in our town considered him a simpleton because he played only children's games and hung around with young boys. He went splashing barefoot in the puddles during a rain, sailed little ships made of matchboxes in the puddles and teased the turkey in Madam Shershenevich's courtyard. The Pechonkies were ready to go through fire and water for him. They loved him more than they loved their own parents. The most aggressive of all his followers was moronic Ignashka, whom we called "Witaway" because when his mother would call him to come home and eat his supper or drink tea, he would answer "Witaway" instead of "right away."

Vaska Pechonkin's favorite occupation was kite flying. He had converted this amusement into a game of plunder. When his kite lifted itself up into the sky, Vaska felt like the master of the heavens. Next to his bird of prey, our kites were like puny sparrows.

Woe betide anyone who dared fly his kite at the same time as Vaska Pechonkin! Pechonkin's kite was as powerful as a giant. With one swing he'd attack the victim, and a desperate sky battle would take place. The smaller kite would be torn off its slender cord and plunge down in broad zigzags, while its owner, bawling like crazy, would race down the street to save the cord, not even trying to get to his defeated kite, lost somewhere in the park or even the sea.

Now, as I was falling asleep, I thought about something I had already thought about a thousand times. Wouldn't it be great if I (together with Vanya Aligeraki and Munya) could build a kite so powerful that it would engage the enemy in the sky and conquer it? If I only had some English twine—would I show Vaska Pechonkin a thing or two! And with this dream, I fell asleep.

# 11

## The Christian Thing,
## The Brotherly Thing

I woke up on Sunday feeling depressed. The great victory over Witaway seemed boring and far away, but the trouble at school was still there inside of me, in every little detail. I jumped out of bed and raced outside without washing up, as far away from my mother as possible.

There was a cellar under our apartment. I lifted its heavy door.

"Where are you going?" Marusya yelled without taking her eyes off her book.

"To see the hedgehog."

But I didn't even look for the hedgehog. I sat down on a broken box and started groaning. What a mess! What a horrible mess! I felt as if there wasn't another person on the face of the earth who was worse off than I, that I would never laugh again in my life. I wanted to lie down in my coffin right now so as not to go on feeling this pain.

I pictured my coffin. It was standing on little short legs

in our living room, diagonally across from the window. It was white with gold tassels, with wreaths and flowers and satin ribbons. And on the ribbons were inscriptions in beautiful lettering.

"TO OUR UNFORGETTABLE PAL,
FROM THE FIFTH-YEAR CLASS OF GYMNASIUM NO. 5"
"TO MY BROTHER, UNTIMELY PERISHED"
"TO MY DEAREST FRIEND, FROM RITA VADZINSKAYA"

There I am, lying in my coffin, and everybody is clustered around looking at me.

"What did he die from?" Madam Shershenevich asks Marusya.

"Akh," she answers. "He was so proud, so noble—and we were *absolutely* unfair to him."

And she presses her tear-soaked handkerchief to her eyes. Only now does she understand what a remarkable brother she had.

At the back of the crowd Six-Eyes and Proshka are standing. Their noses are swollen from crying, their cheeks are gray as clay, their hair is all mussed up, their lips are trembling.

"It's *them*—they're the g-g-guilty parties in his death!" Timosha shouts.

All turn to stare at the guilty parties. They hunch over still more and look furtively out from under their brows. Their eyes are guilty and frightened, like those of a dog who has messed up and knows he's going to be beaten.

"And I too, I too am guilty in his death!" says Father Melety, pulling a clump of hair out of his beard.

And who is that standing by the head of my coffin and

sniveling? It's Zuzya Kozelsky! His tears pour down on
my coffin and water my dead cheeks. "It was Tuntin," he
sobs. "Tuntin made me do it and the poor corpse got all
the blame!"

This vision of my own death gave me a lot of satisfaction. Little by little I calmed down. It's not all lost yet, I
thought to myself. I'll go to see Zuzya and Tuntin. Let
them tell Six-Eyes that the whole thing was their fault.
Six-Eyes is making a mistake. He doesn't know what
really happened, he thinks I'm the worst good-for-nothing
in the whole school. But they're the good-for-nothings,
and I've got to make them come clean.

My tears dried up right away.

That would really be great, by golly!

I jumped up and started pacing around in the dark.
The cellar ended in a cave leading to no one knew where.
This cave had lumps of coal scattered all over it and they
glinted under my feet.

The moment Burgmeister found out it was Tuntin and
not me he should be mad at, he would certainly send
Proshka to see me. Proshka would be drunk. He'd come
up to me and say, "Return to the gymnasium, milord . . .
and be good enough to give your school cap back to me for
a minute. . . ."

And he'd pin a brand-new silver crest on it.

I felt as happy as if all this had actually happened. I
picked up some lumps of coal from the floor and threw
them inside the cave, one after the other. There was a
tinkling noise back there, not exactly like glass or tin.
Somewhere in the back behind the boxes the hedgehog
was snorting.

Yes. I would go see Tuntin and Zuzya Kozelsky. I

would talk them into telling Six-Eyes the truth. And then I'd be a gymnasium student again! I'd go to school and sit down on my bench next to Zuyev. I'd study like the devil. They wouldn't refuse me, no, sir! After all, they wouldn't want to see me go under on account of what they did!

Mama would never find out anything about the whole mess. And then she wouldn't get a headache. Some morning at breakfast—maybe in a month or two, during vacation—I'd mention to her, "You know what? They wanted to kick me out of the gymnasium, by mistake. But now the mistake is all fixed up. I didn't tell you about it at the time, because I didn't want to get you upset over nothing."

I was jumping for joy. I threw handfuls of coal into the cave. I ran out of the cellar, and on the way to the gate I jumped on the iron plate over the garbage pit with both feet. The sound rang out through the court.

"Where are you going?" screamed Marusya.

"Not far. Back soon."

On to Tuntin and Kozelsky! I couldn't go past the Wagner house. The Pechonkies would be lying in wait for me there. Better to take some roundabout route along Old Portofrankovskaya Street.

I raced as if I was going to a fire. I felt that my whole salvation consisted in getting to Tuntin's house on Primorsky Boulevard as fast as I could.

There it was, three stories high, painted bright blue, with a brand-new yellow sign on the gate:

HOUSE OF LIEUTENANT COLONEL'S WIDOW
AGLAYA SEMENOVA TUNTINA.

I dashed up the stone staircase, which had just been repainted to look like marble, and pulled the doorbell handle. Tuntin wasn't up yet. I was ushered into a little room by a housemaid whose face was arrogant and at the same time pitiful, because it was all swollen with toothache. An ugly, baldish old parrot was sitting on a bronze ring in a tall cage and looking at me with bleary contempt. Through the open door to the balcony I could see the distant sea.

I paced back and forth in the little room. I was surrounded by Tuntins. Snapshots of Tuntin on a tricycle, Tuntin in a sailor suit, Tuntin as a five-month-old infant, Tuntin with his mother, Tuntin with his dog.

What are all these Tuntins for? I thought to myself.

In ran a short woman dressed in a red silk Japanese kimono embroidered with gold peacocks. She had no eyebrows at all, and her face was covered with warts. It was Tuntin's mother. All the gymnasium students knew about her because she was madly in love with her son. She took him to school every day—right up to the gates. She would make the sign of the cross over him and give him a kiss. People passing by used to laugh at her. Tuntin himself would make nasty, sullen remarks and disappear inside the gate as fast as possible. He was ashamed that she was his mother, that she was so fat, that she had warts, and that she called him "baby" and "my little sunshine."

"He's so fragile, my little boy!" she would tell everybody. As a matter of fact he was healthy, stupid, sulky and always half asleep.

Even his first name, Valentin, she would pronounce in a special kind of voice, as they do it in French: *Valantan*.

"Valantan is still asleep. He's such a neurasthenic, that boy of mine."

You could hear how proud she was. As if there were

something specially nice about being a "neurasthenic." I wanted to explain why I was there, but she ran up to the pictures hanging on the wall and started telling me about each one.

"Here's Valantan in Ai-Tudor in the Crimea, under his favorite cypress tree. See what a classic profile he has. And here he is in the bathtub, when he was eleven months old. And here he is, at Count Kapnist's Christmas party. And here's Valantan's father, my husband, when he was chief of police in Riga. Looks just like Turgenev,* doesn't he?"

I waited for Madam Tuntina to shut up for one second so I could tell her why I was there. But then she asked me unexpectedly, "And your father . . . tell me . . . is he also a military man?"

"I have no father," I said, turning red in the face.

"What can you mean by that—no father?"

I got even more embarrassed and fell silent. I felt ashamed whenever anybody asked me about my father.

"Where is your father, then? Is he dead?"

"No, he's alive . . . but my mother . . . but I . . . I never saw him."

She knit her powdery eyebrows together.

"What can you mean by that—you've *never* seen him?"

I picked up an ashtray from a little table and twisted it around in my hands.

"Oh, oh, oh!" cried Madam Tuntina, her voice heavy with meaning. She took the ashtray away from me and put it back on the table with a bang. "What do you want from my Valantan?"

"You see," I said, "Six-Eyes . . . I mean our principal . . .

---

* A famous Russian writer.

well, Burgmeister . . . kicked me out of school yesterday because he thinks I egged somebody on to . . . you don't know him, his name is Zuzya Kozelsky . . . egged him on to forge his report card and bury his notebook in the ground. But I didn't have anything to do with it. It was Tuntin who egged him on . . . *your son* . . . Valentin. So I want him to tell Six-Eyes tomorrow . . . I mean Burgmeister . . . that it wasn't fair to kick me out of school."

Madam Tuntina jumped. "Valantan!" she called out. "Valantan! Valantan!"

Out of everything I had told her, she understood only one thing—that I was threatening her "Valantan" with some kind of unpleasantness.

Pouting and sleepy, Tuntin showed up in the doorway.

"Tuntin! Tuntin!" I said. "Your mother doesn't know, so please tell her . . . you've got to tell Six-Eyes and everybody. Because it was all your doing . . . it was you . . . it wasn't me who did it, it was you. . . . And if you don't tell them the truth, Tuntin . . ."

Calmly, he looked me over while I smeared my tears all over my face with my fists, black from the coal in our cellar. He mumbled something and walked out of the room. His mother walked out after him. The sound of her whispering carried to me from the next room.

Finally the two of them came back. They had such kind, affectionate expressions on their faces! Madam Tuntina walked up to me and patted the sleeve of my jacket.

"Stop it now, stop crying. Come on, that's enough now . . . don't . . . don't . . . please! Everything is going to be fine. You'll see."

I looked at her, and a feeling of hope blazed up in my heart again.

"Oh, Valantan—you don't know him—he's such a— how shall I put it—he's so *responsive*—and so we've decided to do the Christian thing, the brotherly thing . . ."

And suddenly she unclenched my fist and shoved a crumpled packet of paper into it.

I stared at the papers. They were ruble notes. There must have been seven or eight of them.

"Take them—they'll come in handy!" said Tuntin.

"*Handy*? Handy for what?"

"You see, my dear," Madam Tuntina said, "you're beginning a new life now. Now that you've left the gymnasium . . ."

"But what do you mean, 'left' the gymnasium? If Tuntin, if Valentin, if he . . . my friend . . ."

"Friend?" Madam Tuntina smiled. "Pardon me, but what kind of a 'friend' are you for my Valantan? He's going to become the Ambassador to Great Britain, just you wait and see . . . he has such connections, such possibilities! And your Mamasha , . . Valantan just told me . . . washes shirts for Madam Shershenevich."

A frenzy took hold of me. I got a wild desire to kick her little marble table over on top of her. I wanted to give Tuntin a slap on his bored cheeks.

In expectation of that slap he covered his "classic profile" with his hands. Madam Tuntina rushed over to me to defend her Valantan, but I pushed both of them away and shoved the pack of ruble notes into the parrot's cage. I ran out of that room repeating over and over to myself, "Oh, you pig-face! You ugly fat pig-face, you!"

# 12

## From House to House

Things aren't hopeless yet, I told myself. On to Kozelsky's! But my cheerful mood had evaporated. I plodded hopelessly over to Vorontsov Park, so stooped over I was practically doubled up.

The Kozelskys lived no more than a few steps away from their restaurant. Their windows looked out on the court. It was a very old court, quiet and shady, paved with blocks of lava rock. It had poplar trees, a fountain and a statue of a naked boy with a swan. There was a little garden in front of the windows. In that garden among the clipped laurel bushes a crowd of people was merrily clustered, peeping inside the windows as if they were watching a wedding.

I walked up to the window, and the first thing I saw was—eyes. Bulging, bloodshot eyes. Terrifying eyes, like two revolvers. The eyes were staring at Zuzya Kozelsky, who was all scrunched up in back of a couch standing crosswise against the wall. I couldn't see Zuzya's face, but even the back of his neck expressed terror. The eyes belonged to his father Sigismund Kozelsky, who looked like a squat gnome—bald, neckless and purple-faced with rage.

All the furniture was pushed out of place. For the first minute you might have thought the father and the son were playing some game. The father was chasing his son through the rooms while the son, running away, kept pushing objects into his father's path—now a chair, now a bookcase, now a folding screen. Seen at a distance, it could pass for a circus act . . . if the father hadn't been so furious, and the son hadn't been so deathly afraid.

Now they were separated by one last barricade—the couch. Every time the father tried to run around it from the right, the son would slide toward the left. And if the father tried to get at him from the left side, the son would turn up on the right. This was repeated again and again, in dead silence.

The crowd was indignant at Zuzya. "Rotten kid! Doesn't want to mind his father!"

Using all the force of his body, shoulders and chest, the father threw himself at the back of the couch, and the couch moved on top of Zuzya and drove him into the corner. Zuzya tried to crawl under it, but his father grabbed him by the pants and dragged him into the middle of the room.

I couldn't watch any more. I closed my eyes. The crowd pressed closer to the windows. I ran over to the gates and saw an elderly yardkeeper sitting on a mound of earth, affectionately petting a big cat which was purring away on his lap.

I'm very bashful, as a rule. I don't like to strike up con-

versations with strange yardkeepers. Yardkeepers, postmen, doormen, policemen and even horsecar conductors
all look official to me. But this yardkeeper was petting his
cat with so much kindliness that I got up the nerve to ask
him to call the police.

"No policeman needed here," he replied. "It's only a
father walloping his kid to put some sense into him. What
do the police have to do with it? That's what fathers
are for."

The old man's eyes were gentle. The cat purred con-
tentedly under his hand.

Slowly, I left for Cathedral Square. I felt sorry for
Zuzya but even sorrier for myself. I understood that Zuzya
was a lost cause. He wouldn't be going to the school principal tomorrow, and he wouldn't tell him the truth about
Tuntin. He was scared to death. It was too late to get any
information out of him. He'd be crying for three days
straight and shivering like a dog.

What on earth was I to do? Where could I go? Whose
advice could I ask? My poor mother! And that Madam
Tuntina, in her peacock kimono. Repulsive wart-face!

The clock on the face of the cathedral showed a quarter to one. That meant I had seventeen hours left. What
could be done in seventeen hours?

And suddenly I got a clear mental picture of Timosha's
face on my last day at school. How upset he was, and
how he had glared at Proshka when Proshka laughed
at me and ripped the silver crest off my cap! Timosha, my
best friend! When I was called to the blackboard he would
turn pale with excitement, and if I was praised for a good
answer he would break out in smiles. How could I have
forgotten him? It was to him I should have gone first, and

only afterward to Zuzya and Tuntin. Even if Timosha couldn't do anything to help me, still he would share my misery, and then things would start looking better. Yesterday in school he had been trying to tell me something, but I hadn't really paid attention. Did he tell me to come and see him?

I remembered that Father Melety and Timosha's father were "fellow countrymen"—both of them far northerners from Arkhangelsk. And soon I started to believe that if Timosha's father would put in a good word for me to Father Melety, Father Melety would take pity on me and I'd . . . I'd be sitting behind my school desk again!

Timosha lived by the seacoast next door to the Customs House. It was a long trip to his place down all the streets and lanes. But there was a shortcut, a steep, clayey slope overgrown with weeds. I made my way through the park to the slope and slid down, head over heels, almost directly to the Customs House.

It must have rained not long before, but I didn't pay any attention. There was the sea, striped with foam. Suddenly I was hit by a cutting, whistling sea wind.

The house where Timosha lived was more like a ship than a house. Long and narrow with a high "poop," it faced the sea and seemed on the point of sailing away. It even had a deck—a wide balcony that wrapped around the entire house. Seagulls were flying over it, and a flag was flapping. The whole house was shaking from the force of the wind and the breakers.

The door wasn't locked. I went down the kitchen steps, which looked like a ship's ladder. Timosha's aunt was usually to be seen bustling around the kitchen, with her hair all done up in curls. Her corset would be creaking and her face would look as if she had just swallowed a glass of vinegar.

But now—what a surprise! The kitchen greeted me with noise and laughter. There were two young girls in it. One of them was Lida Kuryndina, and the other was Timosha's sister, "two-toned Liza." We called her "two-toned" because she had a dark chestnut streak in her bright gold curls, right near her forehead.

The two girls were holding white slippers which they were cleaning with tooth powder. A lamp was burning on the table, and curling irons were lying on top of the lamp. Timosha's father and aunt had both gone off to some farm or other. In the absence of the grown-ups the girls had snitched Auntie's curling irons, powder, pomade, rouge and perfume. Ever since morning they had been curling, rouging and whitening themselves, even though they were both very rosy-cheeked and their hair was curly enough already.

The masquerade gave them the wildest pleasure. They were sh-h-ing each other, squealing and jumping around in fits of the giggles. I had always been curious to know why the girls were always whispering and what they were always giggling about. But right now it was hard for me even to take it in that other people could be having fun when I was feeling so rotten.

"Where's Timosha?" I asked.

"Who knows? He went out. . . . I think he went to see Finti-Monti," Liza answered. Then she took a good look at me and broke out into giggles all over again. "How did you get yourself so filthy? Where have you been?"

It was only now that I noticed that my jacket and pants were thickly smeared with clay.

Liza laughed and took me over to the mirror in her aunt's room. "Look what a scarecrow you are!"

I stared at my dirty suit covered from top to bottom with brown clay stains.

"How can I go outside like this?" I said in bitter despair.

The girls dragged me back into the kitchen, armed themselves with two prickly wet brushes and started cleaning off the clay with four hands. While they were bustling over me and pulling me around, I was thinking all the time about how to reach Timosha. I realized that he must have gone to Finti-Monti to tell him about my disaster and consult with him on what to do.

But then, why wasn't he home yet?

Suddenly the doorbell rang upstairs.

"Oh, that's Timosha!" yelled Liza and dashed up the steps, getting herself all tangled up in her aunt's skirt.

She was a merry, prankish, wisecracking girl. She could row a boat, and swam in all kinds of weather, farther out than anybody else. Lida, who was bossed around dictatorially by her, had a much better disposition than Liza.

"Why do you look so miserable today?" she asked me when the two of us were left alone. "And my goodness— what a mess your hair is! Give me that comb over there, I'll get you fixed up."

Liza came running back in and grabbed one of her aunt's little jars. "Wait a minute! We'll put some rouge on him!"

Then, finally, she saw that I was in no mood for kidding around, and said in a quieter voice, "Timosha was down in the dumps today too. He didn't even get washed. Just drank his tea and ran out."

"But who rang just now? Wasn't it Timosha?"

"No, it was somebody else. Rita."

Rita Vadzinskaya! The blood rushed to my face, my hands started to shake and I ran through the kitchen door. The girls' laughter followed me. They had known about my crush on Rita for a long time now.

I don't remember how I got to the house where Finti-Monti lived. But there too failure was waiting for me. The door was padlocked and both the windows were shuttered tight. Ludwig Meier was sitting underneath a dripping acacia tree and reading some book with his nearsighted German eyes. I always felt awkward around him. He was so smart and so important-looking.

I waited for Meier to finish his chapter and then asked him whether Timosha Makarov from the fifth-year class had been there to see Ivan Mitrofanych. Timosha Makarov, the one with the ears that stuck out. But Meier didn't hear me and didn't pay attention to me. He was completely under the spell of the book he had just finished.

There was no point asking him any more questions. I left quietly. It started to drizzle again.

# 13

## A Very Wise Piece of Advice

I was surrounded by unfamiliar streets, walking, I didn't know where. Finally I sat down on somebody's front steps, closed my eyes and leaned my head against the railing. Vague purple shadows floated past me in a kind of mist, and every shadow was Tuntin. Tuntin on a tricycle, Tuntin on a pony, Tuntin in a sailor suit, Tuntin as a five-month-old infant, Tuntin in a Cherkessian hat.

And then all these Tuntins disappeared, and I lost consciousness. That used to happen to me sometimes when I was little. Once my mother used a needle to take a splinter out of the palm of my hand, and I nearly passed out in her arms. Another time after a very long time in the water, I lay on the baking hot beach for about a quarter of an hour, half conscious. While I was passed out somebody stole the tin bucket I loved, and I moped over it for days afterward.

I woke up in the midst of birds. Birds were standing on shelves in rows. Miniature ostriches no bigger than a little finger, tiny cranes without beaks, roundheaded owls.

"What kinds of birds are those—with the tails—over there?"

"Those are ibises. Sacred Egyptian birds."

It was a strange voice, a remarkably pleasant voice. I heard it, then fell asleep again. When I woke up a conversation was going on in the room.

"Aren't you ashamed of yourself, Papa!" the voice said. "Pooh! It's absolutely disgraceful. Goodness, you've already had four pieces."

There was a guilty mumbling in reply.

"Oh, such a disgrace! What would poor Mama say if she were alive? Pooh! Pooh! I'm so ashamed, so very ashamed of you!"

I half-opened my eyes and saw a very old man, clean-shaven, wearing a green cap with a black tassel on it. He had a long, sharp nose. At the tip of this nose a clean, bright, transparent drop was gradually growing bigger and bigger, and then it fell on the old man's lap. Another drop . . . another . . . for a long time I followed these clear drops with my eyes.

"He's awake!" said the same voice which had just been scolding the old man. "Sister Francesca, is it ready?"

Suddenly I smelled the intoxicating smell of beans. This smell was as inviting as everything else in that room. I breathed it in with deep breaths and raised myself up a little from the couch. I saw two white-haired, pink-cheeked old ladies, as tiny and thin as ten-year-old girls.

Where was I? What was this place?

Seeing that I wasn't asleep, one of the old ladies handed

me a smoking hot plate of soup and a stale heel of grayish bread. I got this down my throat very fast, and was soon staring at a picture at the bottom of the empty bowl. Three poodles with different-colored bows around their necks were sitting and grinning. One of them was winking, as if he knew something funny about me.

It was obvious that the people who lived in this room were crazy about pictures. Even the blanket they had covered me with was embroidered with stars and butterflies. The walls were covered from ceiling to floor with many-colored hangings embroidered with tigers, knights, flowers, anchors and rainbows. Pillows of every shape and color imaginable were ranked by size on the couch, and every pillow had a picture on it: on one, a rose, on another, those very same poodles I had just seen winking at the bottom of my soup bowl, on a third, Robinson Crusoe sitting under an umbrella.

I stared around at the cheerful room, which seemed to be saying, "What nonsense that there should be unhappiness in the world! The world is nothing but soft hangings and many-colored pictures and pillows."

"Sister Malvina, please give me the matchbox."

The matchbox turned out to be inside a dark-blue beaded case. When Sister Francesca climbed up on a chair and lit the big hanging lamp, the silhouettes of Chinese children and men started dancing around on the glass lampshade.

One of the sisters was nimble, quick and talkative and moved like a young woman, while the other, who wore spectacles, seemed older and more stolid. They came from Alsace-Lorraine (as I found out afterward). Mademoiselle Francesca and Mademoiselle Malvina. They had been living in Odessa almost from childhood, and they spoke Russian quite correctly, with a very pleasant foreign accent. Except that instead of saying "as if" they would say *zeef*.

"We were looking out the window and it seemed zeef somebody was lying there. 'Oh my goodness!' I said to sister Francesca. 'It looks zeef he's dead!' "

Their father, Monsieur Ricquet, had once been a dancing teacher. But now he was ninety-six years old and for many years he had been sitting in his easy chair, snuggled up in a warm plaid. Embroidered on it was a black bat, against the background of a giant moon. He was deaf and could hardly see. He had even lost his taste for smoking, which he had loved up to two years before. For days on end he would sit in his chair without saying a word.

But there was one thing in his life that he still loved as much as he ever had—sugar. And since his daughters never gave him as much sugar as he wanted, he would steal it from them at every opportunity. When they realized that he got pleasure out of his stealing, his daughters would purposely put the sugar bowl close to his hand, so that he could steal from it more conveniently. It was funny to watch him looking around like a thief, reaching out his hand for the loot they provided him with. Imagining that he had brought off a daring robbery, he was as happy as a child. The stolen lump of sugar he popped into his mouth and sucked with relish tasted twice as good to him. He was particularly happy when he daughters scolded him with their "Pooh, Papasha, aren't you ashamed of yourself!" When he heard those words he would picture himself as a terrific slyboots and cunning old fox. That would flatter him, and he'd grin with self-satisfaction.

All the while they were telling me about these eccentric

habits of their father, the sisters kept on working without a stop. On the table in front of them lay heaps of scraps and ends of every possible kind of fabric, and they were stitching these things together with different-colored threads. Out of this a red and green and blue patchwork tablecloth was taking shape. I felt like lying on that couch forever and watching their fingers flash. They told me (it was actually Francesca who talked—Malvina only moved her eyebrows in sympathy) that they taught needlework and music in different schools, and on top of that they made birds out of worsted yarn and sold them.

"Watch this!" said Francesca. She picked up her scissors and a playing card. She folded the card into four, cut a little hole like a bagel out of it, drapped it in bright yellow yarn and tinkled her scissors around it. And suddenly a fluffy yellow chicken appeared, looking just hatched.

"What a shame there's no wax for the beak. See how many storks we have without beaks!" said Francesca with a sigh. "The price of wax has gone up so high!"

"Simply awful!" sighed Malvina. "And that no-good Subbotsky—"

I knew Subbotsky. He lived in our court and had a stationery shop across the street from the Kroll Gymnasium for Girls. He would smile sweetly at his trusting little customers, pat them on the head and call them "kiddie."

But never mind all that. The man was a swindler. According to Francesca and Malvina, he would buy their owls, ostriches, chickens and storks for next to nothing and then sell them to the stores at a huge profit to himself. He paid the sisters ten kopecks for each chicken and received fifty for it. And the stores would sell these chickens for a ruble apiece, because "Subbotsky's chickens" were famous for their beauty. That was just what they were called—"Subbotsky's chickens." People would buy them up like hot cakes, especially around Easter and Christmas time. And meanwhile the materials for making the birds were getting so expensive that the sisters were left with no more than two and a half kopecks per chicken.

"I'll get you some wax!" I said. "I'll tell my Uncle Foma and he'll bring it from the country. He has honey and bees in his house in the country. He has pounds and pounds of wax!"

And then I told them about Uncle Foma. And then about my mother, about Six-Eyes and about my trouble. They listened. Suddenly Malvina said, "You go straight to your mother and tell her the whole truth. So it will hurt her, will it? Then let it! Pain is better than lies. Even death is better than lies. Go tell your mother the truth, and you'll see—everything will come out right."

I was all mixed up. I couldn't understand why, if they felt that way about telling the truth, they kept on deceiving their father about the sugar. But the minute I started hinting at this, Francesca interrupted me.

"Oh, Papa—that's a different matter entirely! With Papasha—it's zeef he's only a two-year-old child."

I jumped to my feet. "All right! I'll go to her and tell her."

"And send your mother, from us—from Francesca and Malvina—our love. And this too, please."

And she took a red-breasted woodpecker off the shelf, put it into a little paper bag (the paper bag also had a picture painted on it) and handed it to me.

I rushed home feeling as if I was flying. It was only

then that I realized what a heavy load it had been to hide the truth from my mother all this time.

But then why did they give me the woodpecker? Was it to give my mother pleasure now, just when I'd be telling her the truth about our disaster?

# 14

## A Breathing Spell

I wanted so much to tell my mother every little detail—
Zuzya, Tuntin, Six-Eyes, Proshka, the silver crest,
every single thing that had happened during these days. I
even wanted her to know about Witaway, even about
Filimon the goat. So that when I walked into our room
and saw nobody there but Marusya, I was ready to burst
with frustration.

No Mama in the kitchen, no Mama in the cellar.

I had been running away and hiding from her for so
long! And now I felt I would give anything in the world to
press my cold, wet face against her roughened hands.

Marusya stared at me coldly, as if to say: do pitiful
beings like you really exist, who go running around God
knows where for days at a time? I felt guilty toward her
(that was my usual feeling toward her) and I asked her in
a barely audible voice where Mama was. In her distinct
diction Marusya answered that I should stop pretending

to be a fool, since I knew perfectly well that Uncle Foma had left for the country today at noon, and that Mama had gone to the Ackermann Gate to see him off.

So I was a genuine criminal! Our family had a long-standing tradition that whenever Uncle Foma left, Mama and I would go to say goodbye to him at the Ackermann Gate, and afterward we would drop in to see Long Liza. Long Liza always said to me, "Oy-oy—how you've grown, knock on wood!" And then she would run to the shop and bring back some gingerbread cookies covered with flies and hard as a rock; and I would break my jaw gnawing on those gingerbreads all the way home.

Long Liza felt very grateful to my mother because once, long ago, when there was a pogrom against the Jews in our town, Mama hid her in our cellar in a tub and covered her over with cabbage. We still had the tub, and it was always known as "Liza's tub."

And here my mother had gone to the Ackermann Gate alone, without me. And Uncle Foma was gone, and I didn't have a chance to kiss him on his moustache smelling of bread and cherry brandy, and I didn't even see what goodies Mama had bought for his wife and children. Though these goodies were almost always the same: half a sugarloaf, a quarter pound of tea, some sticky candies wrapped up in paper and called "Tsar's Bouquet," and a length of blue or yellow calico bought on sale at Ptashnikov's store.

I stood in front of Marusya, embarrassed. "Look at this, Marusya!"

I showed her the paper bag with the picture and took out the woodpecker Mademoiselle Francesca had given me. Not until now did I see how beautiful it was. A section of tree trunk had been sculpted out of brick-colored clay. It was complete down to the bark and the knots in the wood. On this trunk the woodpecker was perched, pecking at the trunk with his long beak, modeled from the best quality wax.

"It's mine . . . it's for Mama—they gave it to me. . . ."

But Marusya only stared at the woodpecker antagonistically, as if the woodpecker too was guilty toward her and Mama and Uncle Foma.

I went into the kitchen. I had chills and fever. I must have caught a cold. It would be nice to drink a glass of hot tea. In the barracks across the street there was a tank—a big boiler cemented to a hot plate. Some soldier would take my kopeck and pour me a potful of scalding tea from the tank. I picked up the teapot from the kitchen table and noticed a note lying under it.

COME TO DRAKONDIDI'S TONIGHT AT TEN.
VERY IMPORTANT MATTER! (signed) BLOKHIN.

I ran outside, bending over as I passed the windows, so that Marusya wouldn't see me.

I had never been to Drakondidi's. Drakondidi's was the secret meeting place for our gymnasium club. All the students knew this club existed, but they talked about it only in whispers. It was where the second-year students Zuzulya and Kutz drank vodka out of kvass bottles. Where the Babenchikov brothers played their card game called give-it-to-the-jackass. Sasha Bugai used to go there whenever he managed to snitch a three-ruble note from his father. He would eat meat pies and ice cream, and even treated Zuyev and his brother.

Drakondidi's was the place where the kids who played

hookey went to hide from our class supervisor. "The hooks"—that was our name for the fellows who hung around outside of school (usually in the park or at the seashore) when they were supposed to be in class. If someone didn't prepare his physics assignment and was sure to get a mark of 1, he'd leave home with his schoolbag just as if he was going to the gymnasium. But he'd walk two or three streets, then sneak off to some secret place where he'd spend the day. And then he'd go home and lie to his parents without turning a hair. The hooks with money spent their days at Drakondidi's, where they stuffed themselves with food and drinks, played cards, lotto or dominoes, and just slept.

And the peculiar thing about it was that nobody had ever been caught red-handed in Drakondidi's by the school officials, although there were times—say on a day when there was some specially hard lesson—when up to a dozen students were gathered there. They would even set it up in advance: "Tomorrow the whole crowd will be at Drakondidi's from morning on."

Once Sasha Bugai invited our entire class to Drakondidi's. It was the last class of the day, French. After the lesson we were supposed to read a prayer. "We thank You, our Creator, for enabling us to receive Your grace in hearing our lessons. Bless our leaders, our parents and teachers, leading us to the knowledge of good. . . ."

Sasha Bugai stepped forward. Exploiting the fact that Monsieur Lan didn't understand a word of Russian, he said, in the same singsong voice they used for reciting prayers in church: "Unto them who don't wish to get a zero in Greek, may they pinch half a ruble from their folks and hide out in the thieves' den of Dra-kon-di-di!"

Then he gazed piously at the icon and crossed himself.

Lan lowered his eyes reverently in order to show that he respected other people's religious faith.

I had heard a lot more stories about Themistocles Drakondidi and his "thieves' den" from Munya Blokhin, who played chess there every Friday with the student Iglitsky from the Science School.

I didn't know quite where I was running. It was only a quarter to eight, still too early to go there. I wondered if I ought to go see Vanya Aligeraki, my neighbor, who had a white rat and a pair of new tumbler pigeons. No. I wasn't in the mood for pigeons and white rats. Maybe I should go back to Mademoiselle Francesca and Mademoiselle Malvina's, and listen for a while to their funny *zeef*.

Undecidedly, I walked out of the gate. The street was deserted. Not a soul. If only Rita Vadzinskaya would appear! I noticed Top Hat standing at our gate, dressed to kill in a blinding bright purple necktie. The smell of cologne was enough to knock you over. He didn't say hello, just pulled a little box out of his pocket and held up a silver heart pierced by a white arrow. A blue stone was set inside the heart.

"Elegant little toy, that!" he said triumphantly. "You think she'll like it?"

*She*—that was redheaded Celia, the wrapper in Gluzman and Romm's candy factory. For about a year now, Top Hat had been out of his mind with love for this pretty girl. It was for her that he had become a snappy dresser. Even his way of walking was changed. Before, he would walk like a cat, cautious and stealthy—but now it was more like a kind of skipping, almost dancing.

I tried to pay attention to what he was telling me. What

a piece of luck to have bumped into him! I could talk to him, and push my miseries away for another half hour. So unbearable was the load dumped on my shoulders that I thanked fate from the bottom of my heart for this chance to talk to Top Hat. I needed that breathing spell. I was so scared he might go away and leave me alone that I started working up a hot interest in Top Hat's affairs.

We sat down on a bench by the entrance gate. Again, Top Hat took the pin with the blue stone out of his pocket.

"I bet you think I stole it, don't you? Just look at this!" Triumphantly he showed me a slip of paper, a receipt from the jewelers Bise and Company. On the receipt was written: "Silver brooch. 3 rubles 48 kop." And under this line was the round stamp of the shop.

"Look at that stamp there, oho-ho! It's the genuine article, may God strike me down!"

He seemed amazed himself to realize that he hadn't stolen the pin.

I knew Celia wouldn't accept any present from him without that stamp. As soon as they got to know each other she made him stop stealing and promise never again to work at his "specialty." And he really did stop. As a matter of fact, Top Hat hadn't stolen a thing for more than a year. Mama had advised him to study "lathe turning" in the Kaiser furniture factory on the corner of Kanatnaya and Novaya. Now he was an apprentice there, and people didn't call him Top Hat any more but addressed him as Yosif or Yuzya Stock (or maybe it was Stockmann). Whenever anybody called him Top Hat, he would get insulted.

He had assured Mama and me long ago that he had

stopped stealing. But we never really believed him until now. He brought his Celia to visit us a couple of times, and was terribly happy to see how much we liked her. He still came to us every Sunday, as always, to fill up our water barrels, clean the beets and potatoes for Mama for supper, hang out the wash in the loft together with Malanka and run to the library to fetch books for Marusya.

Good old Top Hat! What a pleasure it was for me to go to the market with him early in the morning when the church bells were chiming for matins. The market would be filled with the hubbub peculiar to the south of Russia. Peddlers would shout, piglets would squeal, everybody haggled with a passion. We would buy live crabs, mackerels, bagels, cherries, halvah. All worn out, we'd head for home. Suddenly Top Hat would burst out laughing. "Those peddlers are asleep on their feet!" And he'd pull a bunch of stuck-together prunes out of his sleeve.

I'd stare at him.

"Yuzya! But you promised! You gave your word of honor. Aren't you ashamed of yourself? Yuzya, Yuzya!"

"You call this stealing?" he would smile, and take out from under his shirt a handful of mealy pearlike medlars, dried apples, cucumbers or caramels. "And naturally you wouldn't care for a slice of dried apple—would you?"

I have to admit that the goodies stolen by Top Hat tasted so super-delicious to me that I was ready not to count them as stolen goods, and would have eaten up the medlars and the prunes and the dried apples without a pang of guilt.

But redheaded Celia was made of sterner stuff. When Top Hat once pinched her favorite chestnuts from the market, she dropped them like hot coals and announced that she didn't care to have anything more to do with such an "incurable pickpocket."

From that day on, when Top Hat went strolling among the fruit stalls on a Sunday, he no longer snitched anything, not even the pumpkin and watermelon seeds from old half-witted Maryanka, who couldn't defend herself even from the little kids who pounced on her from time to time and devastated the contents of her basket. It was funny to watch Top Hat trying to keep his light-fingered hands off the sweets that were lying around, or to see him absentmindedly lift a cucumber or an onion, then realize what he was doing, let out a curse word and throw the thing back into the peddler's sack.

He even cursed less than he used to. My mother ordered him not to use any more foul language. He promised. But the problem was that he didn't know at first which words were "bad" and which were all right. Without turning a hair he could say things that would make a tree blush. But if he happened to say a word like, for instance, "spit" or "pants" or "nuts to you" he would stammer, get very embarrassed and say, "Uh, sorry about that, I apologize!"

But even this department was in perfect working order by now. It was hard to remember that people used to think of him as an "incurable pickpocket." These days even Simonenko the cop didn't doubt Top Hat's honesty.

Top Hat got up. Unfortunately the time had come for him to leave. Celia was waiting for him in the park at the monument to Tsar Alexander II.

"I'm going to Drakondidi's!" I told him, wanting to pour out all my troubles to him.

But he wasn't in the mood to listen any more. He was rushing to meet his Celia. As I sat there on the bench alone, all my misery rolled back on top of me. What was waiting for me in Drakondidi's cellar?

# 15

## Drakondidi's

This cellar was located at the Artificial Mineral Waters Establishment on Uspenskaya Street, opposite the horsecar barn. Lit up by tongues of bluish yellow gas, its white and blue sign sparkled from far away—TH. M. DRAKONDIDI, ARTIFICIAL SODA WATERS AND SYRUPS. On the sign was a painted siphon with water sprinkling out of it in the shape of a fan. I pushed the door open and walked in. The bell sounded louder than I expected.

The first thing I saw was the black beard of Drakondidi himself, a thick, square, Assyrian-looking beard. It looked dyed. Fleshy, bright red lips protruded from it. Drakondidi was standing behind his counter, cleaning some tin spoons with chalk. In front of him on a tall metal pivot were glass geysers full of different flavors of syrup: pineapple, chocolate, cherry, vanilla, raspberry, orange and even something with the strange name of "tulip." This multicolored colonnade of syrups was crowned with a bouquet of paper flowers.

But where was the "club"? Where was that fabulous secret room Munya Blokhin had told me so much about? There was nothing that looked like a door behind Drakondidi's back. A blank wall with a rug hanging on it. And on the rug, a poster:

---

## MANUEL HERZOG CIRCUS
### The Fernando Brothers and Tanti Badini

---

"With syrup or without?" Drakondidi asked me, throwing a spoon into a tall glass.

"No, I don't want any . . . I . . . something else . . . Munya Blokhin told me to come here."

Drakondidi drew his eyebrows together. "What's that you say? Blokhin?"

"From the fifth-year class. From Gymnasium No. 5. Munya."

"Blokhin . . . that's his last name? You're sure it isn't Marazli or Ralli?" (Marazli and Ralli were prominent local merchants.)

"No, Blokhin. You know him. Munya—he plays chess here with that . . . with Iglitsky. I know all the guys who hang out here—Kutz, Zuzulya, the Babenchikov brothers."

"Goddam it, you must be some kind of a nut!" said Drakondidi. "I sell lemonade and syrups here, and this character comes around looking for some Kutz and Zuzulya!"

Could I have made a mistake? Munya had told me that

this whole business of the Artificial Mineral Waters Establishment was nothing but a front, and that the real action went on in back.

I went outside again, stood for a long time under an acacia tree and kept staring stupidly at a gate on which somebody had scribbled in chalk, "Yura loves Raya Gluzman."

The candy factory of Gluzman and Romm was next door to Drakondidi's. Down below, in the basement of this factory, forty or fifty women workers sat behind the barred windows. In that terrible stifling closeness, behind a long, sticky table, swaying back and forth in rhythm and working with the speed of robots, these women wrapped caramel candies in little papers printed "Tsar's Rose. Mfd. by Gluzman and Romm." This was the factory where our redheaded Celia worked, and I couldn't even begin to figure out how she could still laugh after such a long, hard working day, and sometimes even have enough energy left to dance with Top Hat until they were both ready to fall down.

I bent over and looked through the rails, made of water pipes, into the basement window. But today was Sunday, and the factory was closed. Beyond the windows was nothing but blackness. I turned around and saw—Munya Blokhin.

"Munya," I said, "is there another Drakondidi's?"

But Munya only smirked, said his favorite word, "Pfah!" and led me back inside the Artificial Mineral Waters Establishment. He put two twenty-kopeck coins on the counter, one for himself and one for me. And to my amazement Drakondidi greeted him like on old friend. He looked around and then lifted up the hanging, that very hanging with the circus poster attached to it. Behind the hanging there was a low door papered over with torn oilcloth.

"Watch out for the step!" said Drakondidi, and I stumbled forward into a dark semi-basement room. It smelled like smoke, fish, kerosene, dampness and a toilet.

After my eyes got used to the dark, I noticed a shaggy-haired fellow frying fish on the oil stove. Munya told me this was Drakondidi's brother Zhorka, a deaf-and-dumb plumber or locksmith. I had already heard some gossip about him. On the wall over to the right was a curtain. An iron ventilator was scraping away somewhere. Or was it water dripping from a faucet?

So this was it, the famous Club Drakondidi I had heard so much about! For some reason, I was sure it would be all velvet and gilt. And the truth was—greasy tables, sunflower-seed shells, filth, and what a stink!

Munya and I sat down in a far corner. A cockroach ran along the top of our table. Looking around, I caught sight of the Babenchikov brothers. They were sitting by the wall to my right on upturned barrels and shuffling a deck of cards, waiting for partners.

Zhorka handed us two glasses of muddy tea on a rusty black tray and a few little salted hard crackers, the kind they usually serve you with beer.

"That Zhorka—he's some artist, ai-ai-ai!" said Munya, giving me a wink. "For three cigarettes he'll swallow down that cockroach—even two cockroaches."

"What do cockroaches have to do with anything?" I said. "You sent for me. Here I am. And you go on driveling about cockroaches . . . cigarettes . . ."

Munya laughed. "Relax, everything is going to come

out fine. Timosha and I got an idea. Or rather, it was Timosha's idea. It's fantastic! You'll see. He's coming right away. He'll tell you all about it."

There was something unreal about Munya's smile. Or maybe he was just absentminded? I looked at him and realized that he wasn't even thinking about me but had something else entirely on his mind. That was the kind of flighty personality he had. He had already gotten up from the table and run over to Ludwig Meier, trying to sell him a lottery ticket.

"The prize is a famous book. *The Queen's Jewels*, by Alexandre Dumas! Four hundred and twenty pages!"

Then he ran over to Zenkevich, a stamp collector, and exchanged a Cuba for a Java. After that he stopped by the wall opposite the door to play a game of pitch and toss with somebody. From there he went over to a table where Sasha Bugai was eating chocolate halvah, and sang an excited song with him about our class supervisor, waving a bagel around like a conductor's baton the whole time. There wasn't a single person in that room he could pass by without getting involved. Everybody needed him for something, and he needed everybody. The whole room was ringing with "Munya! Munka! Blokhin! Blokha! Over here!"

Now he was approached by Iglitsky, and the two of them sat down to play a game of chess.

My head started to ache from hunger and smoke fumes. I couldn't tear my eyes away from the door. I was sure that the minute I caught sight of Timosha's freckled face, my head would stop aching.

How would he look when he walked in, happy or downcast? And what news would he have for me?

A sliver of light showed in the dark wall where the oilcloth-papered door was.

"Check!" said Iglitsky.

"Check and mate!" said Blokhin, jumping up because Timosha had appeared on the top step.

We ran to him.

It turned out that Drakondidi hadn't wanted to let him in, and that he got through the door practically by force. He gave me a big smile, as always, but his eyes were anxious. His red hair was dark with sweat.

We sat down by the curtain on a pile of bast matting that stank of fish, and Timosha started to describe everything he had been doing since early morning.

"First of all—this was on Munya's advice—I ran to see Emmanuel Beetle."

"My God! What does Beetle have to do with anything?"

Everybody in our school knew Emmanuel Beetle, the barber at the Primorskaya Hotel. What kind of help could be expected from him?

"What are you talking about!" Munya jumped on me. "Or don't you know that he goes to Six-Eyes' apartment every morning before school to give him a shave and a haircut?"

"So what?"

"So this is what. He's the one person with the chance to talk to Six-Eyes every single day!"

Timosha interrupted Munya to describe how graciously this important barber had received him, and how willing he was to put in a word on my behalf.

"Well, that's great!" said I.

"No! J-j-just l-l-listen to the end of the s-s-story!" And Timosha's lower lip started to tremble.

From the rest of his story I realized that Beetle the barber didn't intend to use his influence free of charge. He wanted a hundred rubles for his "conversation" with Six-Eyes. A hundred rubles for one conversation! And if the conversation was a success, the price would be two hundred.

"So what did you expect?" Munya smirked. "That's why he's a Beetle. He's a secret agent for Six-Eyes. Do you think Zuyev and Zozelsky could last in our gymnasium for a single hour if their parents didn't give Beetle a payoff to hand over to Six-Eyes? And not two hundred, not three hundred, but thousands!"

"The hell with Beetle!" I yelled.

Timosha looked at me. He seemed ashamed that his efforts hadn't led to anything. He started telling me how he had gone from Beetle over to Father Melety at Pokrovskaya Church quite a distance away, that he had stood there waiting for him till midday mass was over. And that the moment Father Melety heard the sound of my name, he snorted at him.

I couldn't listen any more. I have to admit that I didn't feel at all grateful to Timosha. Here was a guy who hadn't had anything to eat or drink the whole day, who had been running around the entire city of Odessa for my sake, taking all kinds of trouble for me, and I was listening to him with impatience and irritation, even with spite. I knew the whole time that I was wrong, and that made me feel even more annoyed at him.

"And then I went to see Mitrofanych—Finti-Monti . . ."

"I know! I know all about it! Stop dragging it out!" I said. "I know—you went to see Finti-Monti, *and he wasn't at home.*"

"No, he wasn't," Timosha answered. "So I went to the breakwater and then down to the lighthouse where he fishes for bullheads on holidays. And from there—"

"I don't give a damn where you went. The point is that you didn't find him! Didn't find him! Didn't find him!"

I felt so miserable that I thought it gave me the right to be mean. I grabbed somebody's knobby walking stick and banged it on the table. I started yelling in a surly, hysterical voice that didn't even seem to be coming out of me and that was repulsive to me.

"All of you can go straight to hell! Hell! Hell!"

And then suddenly I came back to myself. "Don't be mad at me . . . I understand . . . I'm sorry . . . But what am I going to do? I can't . . ."

I was choking with tears and I pressed my face against the curtain. It was saturated with the smell of fish.

"Ekh, what a shame we couldn't turn Finti-Monti up!" said Munya. "He'd have advised us, he'd know what to do."

And at that very second we heard the old familiar stream of names. "Blockheads! Penny-whistlers! Loudmouths!"

We jumped to our feet. Finti-Monti! Could he really be here with us?

We ran behind the curtain. Yes, it was Finti-Monti himself, lying on a narrow bench, covered with his shabby overcoat and with half a liter of liquor and a guttering candle sitting on top of his suitcase.

A miracle! How had he managed to turn up here in all this crummy filth and stink? It's true there was a rumor among us students that he sometimes used to drown his sorrows in wine. But I was so used to seeing him sober and important in class behind the teacher's lectern during our history lesson that I literally couldn't believe my eyes.

He raised himself, sat up and smoothed his long moustaches as if he was trying to make up his mind whether to wake up or go on sleeping. And it looked as if he was deciding to go back to sleep. He stretched out his coat to wrap himself up again.

We cried out in a chorus, "Hello, Ivan Mitrofanych!" just like in school.

"Hi there, you poor slobs!" he answered, still half asleep.

I rushed over to him. "What should I do, Ivan Mitrofanych? They expelled me from school—you know about it. Is it true they won't forgive me, that they're not going to let me back in? Honest to God, I'm going to be different from now on! I'll . . ."

Ivan Mitrofanych didn't say a word at first. Then he said, "Oh? So they ex-pelled you?" He rapped it out syllable by syllable. "Well, I have news for you, brother. They expelled me too."

And suddenly he grabbed me by the belt and pulled me toward him. "You're as blind as a bat," he said. "You're not a little boy any more. It's high time for you to understand. . . . Do you really think they kicked you out of school because you played some silly joke on the priest, or with that . . . that Kozelsky? Rubbish and lies! It's not because you were guilty of anything that they drummed you out, it's because you're not *good enough* for them— you're *low-class*. And that's your whole sin. Can't you get it through your head?"

All at once the deaf-and-dumb Zhorka Drakondidi materialized in our corner and began fussing noisily about.

"You think he's really deaf and dumb?" Munya whispered. "Oho-ho! His ears are as good as yours. All day he goes poking around the tables, and tomorrow he'll run to the authorities to inform."

Ivan Mitrofanych got up, took his hat out of his suitcase and threw his cape over his shoulders. I handed him his knobby walking stick, the one I had been banging on the table, and he started walking toward the door.

"No, get back! Not that way!" Munya shouted, leading us into a little side closet. Just as if we were climbing out of a putrid well, we scrambled up until we were outside under the sky. In front of us were trees, bushes, the silhouette of a dovecote. And in another minute we found ourselves in a deserted lane, filled to overflowing with gold moonlight and the shadows of little houses.

# 16

## By the Light of the Moon

We walked along in the moonlight as the biggest moon I had ever seen shone over the city. Finti-Monti abruptly sat down on a stone in the shadow of a house, and again pulled me toward him, repeating his rebuke. "You're not a little boy any more—you're old enough to understand the situation!"

Then he was quiet. Suddenly he asked me, "Didn't you ever hear about the Great Bear? Great Bear the Third, I mean."

"What Great Bear are you talking about?"

"About our Late Great Bear, now 'resting in the Lord.' He's the one that's responsible for your troubles."

"Resting in the Lord." That was how they used to refer to Tsar Alexander III, who had died two years earlier. I remember when the news came to our gymnasium that the Tsar was "resting in the Lord," or in plain language, dead. Right away Six-Eyes, Proshka and Father Melety started praising the dead Tsar. They pounded themselves on the chest and told us so many times what a kind, wise and noble Tsar he had been, that finally we school kids began to believe it, and we felt terrible about our loss. The portrait of him hanging in our auditorium, with its frame all draped in black cloth, showed such a kindhearted face that when you looked at it you would never imagine him capable of pulling any dirty tricks on people.

But the real truth, according to Finti-Monti, was that this Tsar of ours had behaved like a bullying policeman or an Army drillmaster. Together with his ministers he had drawn up a vicious law which came to be known as the "Decree of the Cooks' Children." This decree stated that the children of workers, artisans, coachmen, dishwashers, store clerks, draymen, seamstresses and so forth were not to be admitted to the gymnasium under any circumstances.

"But why would it make the Tsar happy," I asked, "for us to stay ignorant?"

Munya broke in before Finti-Monti could answer.

"Just tell me, now," he said mockingly, "why would it make the Tsar happy to see you as a university student? What good would that be to him? Rich people don't go around making riots and rebellions, but poor people—and working people at that—oho-ho!"

"True, true," said Finti-Monti. Leaning heavily on his cane, he walked into a strip of moonlight.

"Now he's going to give us a song! Just you wait," whispered Munya to me. "I know him by now. Pfah!"

And he was right. Finti-Monti gave a little cough, then started singing the song of the barge haulers in a husky baritone: *"Ai-yukh-nyem."*

## By the Light of the Moon

*Go out to the Volga. Whose groan rings out*
*O'er the mighty Russian river?*
*This groan that we call a song . . .*

Then he broke off. Grabbing me by the belt, he repeated over and over that none of what had happened was my fault, that there was nothing to blame myself for, that I had nothing to do with the whole episode. I couldn't understand every detail of what he was saying, but I took in the main part of it. The problem wasn't whether or not I had egged Kozelsky on to bury his school notebook. The point was that my mother didn't own a house as Tuntin's mother did nor any bathhouses or taverns as Zuyev's mother did, nor any shops like the Babenchikovs', nor a restaurant like Sigismund Kozelsky's. My mother owned nothing but her own two hands, rough to the point of bleeding from washing other people's dirty clothes. That was the real reason for making sure I would never occupy a student's bench at the university.

"Why do you keep putting yourself down, scraping and bowing to them!" said Ivan Mitrofanych. "It's as plain as the nose on your face. They've handed Six-Eyes an order from the top—get rid of half a dozen 'cooks' children' from the gymnasium. So he aimed his artillery and picked off seven boys: you, Finkelstein, Yakovenko, Christopoulos, and the ones from the sixth-year class. It wasn't so hard for him to find your weak spots, rest assured! He gets his orders and he carries them out."

We began walking, passing shops, houses, front yards. Kanatnaya Street, so familiar to me, looked strange and poetic in the moonlight. You couldn't recognize a single house. We seemed to be on another planet.

Finti-Monti grabbed me by the belt again. "But those traitors won't be lording it over us much longer!

*The cocks are crowing in Holy Russia;*
*Day will soon dawn in Holy Russia!"*

His words had an exhilarating effect on me. Enough of this putting myself down, scraping and bowing! I wasn't guilty of anything! And that was just what I would tell my mother. I'd explain the whole thing to her. It was they who were guilty, guilty toward *me*—yes . . . yes!

I started telling Finti-Monti about the barber Emmanuel Beetle. "He's Six-Eyes' right-hand man," Finti-Monti confirmed. "He works for him on a percentage basis."

According to what he told me, our principal was the most notorious bribe taker of them all. When the people of our town wanted to say the worst thing they could about somebody who was looking for a payoff, they would say "He skins you like Burgmeister." Trading in school grades was a real business with him. He even had a fixed price. So much for a 3, more for a 4, even more for a 5. Especially during the last quarter, when the report of the whole year's school results was compiled. Finti-Monti had tried to expose this practice wherever he could. He had even written an article about it for the newspapers—but the government censor wouldn't pass it. He then wrote up a document and sent it to the Minister of Education. And from him he had received this answer: "Drop it."

"B-b-but tell me then," Timosha stuttered. "Why does the minister love Six-Eyes, if he's really such a cannibal?"

Finti-Monti was too tired to answer, so Munya answered

for him. "Didn't you ever notice how Six-Eyes sings 'God Save the Tsar'? How he crosses himself and kisses all the icons? How he sniffles whenever he mentions the name of the Tsar's poor widow, Empress Maria? That's exactly the attitude the ministry is looking for. For that, they're ready to forgive even bigger things!"

Deeply absorbed in my talk with Finti-Monti, I hadn't noticed that we had come to my own gateway.

"Goodbye," Finti-Monti said. "And remember this: you may be an outcast, you may be a plebeian. But you're not a slave!"

Top Hat ran out to meet me as I entered the passageway. He was jumping around, waving his hands and shouting like a madman so the whole street could hear.

"Here he is! Here he is! He's back! Alive! And didn't even dream of drowning himself."

Suddenly I was surrounded by Mama and Marusya and Malanka and Long Liza and Celia—all of them noisily rejoicing over my safe return.

Little by little I began to take it all in. It seemed that when my mother came home and didn't find me there, she grew worried. She was even more worried when she spied Munya's note on the kitchen table telling me to go to Drakondidi's. Neither Mama nor Marusya had the faintest idea who or what Drakondidi was. Then Top Hat arrived, read the note and rushed over to Uspenskaya Street (he had been at Drakondidi's himself more than once). I had already left there, which upset Mama even more. Had I drowned myself in the sea, the way the two seminary students Fyuk and Zharov had done a few days ago?

Timosha and Munya Blokhin had walked on. I wanted to catch up to them and say thanks, but Top Hat didn't let me. Now that I was back home safe and sound, Mama ordered me to go and give myself a good washing up first of all. I took soap and a sponge and went with Top Hat behind the barn, where he mercilessly poured cold water over me.

Inside, a bowl of borshch was waiting for me on the table, but I wasn't in any shape to touch food. A few minutes later, when the outsiders left, I began telling my mother disjointedly about everything I had been hiding from her all this while.

"You don't know . . . I give you my word of honor . . . it wasn't me, it was Tuntin . . . and then Father Melety . . . and the Tsar . . . Finti-Monti says—please listen to me!"

My mother looked at me with a strange, quiet smile. It was obvious that she hadn't guessed a thing. It could never have entered her head that I had been deceiving her yesterday and today, that all the money she had paid out for my gymnasium education, for my notebooks and textbooks, for the schoolbag with the fuzzy cover, and the round pencil case, and the gymnasium uniform with the shiny buttons—that all that money, earned by drudgery, was wasted, thrown out. The same as if it had been pitched into the fire.

"Mama, I have to tell you . . . Six-Eyes . . . yesterday . . . no, the day before yesterday . . ."

"I know all about it," said my mother. "I've known for a long time."

My heart stopped. "You know?"

"Ever since yesterday morning. A document arrived from the Gymnasium. Early in the morning, on Saturday, while Uncle Foma was here."

So then it was all for nothing! All for nothing that I ran away, all for nothing that I pretended everything was all right! At the moment when I was sitting in class and hiding behind Munya Blokhin's back, my mother already knew about the calamity that had taken place.

And yet she hadn't mentioned a word of this to Uncle Foma or Marusya. And now she calmly fished out a carefully folded sheet of paper from behind the stove and handed it to me. On it was written in the most elegant handwriting:

> The Pedagogical Council of Odessa Gymnasium No. 5 informs you, esteemed madam, that by a resolution of the Council, your son is expelled from the fifth-year class of the above-named gymnasium for lack of progress in his studies and for pernicious influence on the other students. Kindly be good enough to appear at the bursar's office of the gymnasium to receive the documents appertaining to your expelled son. Receive, esteemed madam, our assurances of deep respect and devotion,
>
> A. Burgmeister, Principal
> Gymnasium No. 5

This document was a death sentence for my mother and me. And yet my mother remained calm. She didn't call me a bum or a loafer, the way Marusya loved to do. If only she would yell at me, or even cry! There was something frightening about her numbness. I grabbed her hands, cold as if they were dead, and begged her over and over again, "Don't, don't! Please don't! Please listen to me! Finti-Monti explained the whole thing to me today. . . ."

I told her everything we had been discussing out on the street in the moonlight. After that I told her about the Ricquet sisters, and about Kozelsky and Tuntin. And then we both quieted down and just sat there on the long trestle bed in the kitchen for a long time.

The lamp started to waver and then went out. The room seemed to grow lighter after that. The whole kitchen was full of moonlight.

In an agitated voice, my mother told me a story I had never heard before. It was the story of her own life with my father, who deserted her in Petersburg after I was born. And finally, she stopped talking.

It wasn't till then that I realized my face was all wet with tears. But inside, I felt as light as if there had never been any Father Melety in the world, or Six-Eyes, or Proshka, or Educational Trustee von Lustig. I put my head down on my mother's lap and, patting her hands gently, I fell asleep.

# 17

## Monday

On Monday I slept till noon and woke up with such a tremendous appetite as I had never felt in my life before. I threw myself wolfishly on my food, ate an enormous bun sprinkled with poppy seeds and finished off last night's bowl of borshch. I drank so much tea that Marusya said, "You really are abnormal, I swear!"

Maybe I was abnormal. From the minute I understood that I really and truly was not guilty of doing anything wrong, that it was the school principal and his "arch-angels," as Finti-Monti called them, who were making me shoulder the blame for everything, and—most important of all—that I didn't have to be afraid of my mother or hide from her any more, a fantastic feeling of freedom and lightness took hold of me.

I ran outside. In a couple of minutes I climbed the rope up to my Wigwam, jumped up on the barrel and dug out the poem I had written from its secret hiding place. It was

written inside a tattered school notebook with a blue cover
and a title lettered on the front.

### GYMNASIADA
*An Epic Poem in Twelve Parts*
*With an Epilogue*

On the first page, carefully lettered and outlined in red
ink, was the line:

---

DEDICATED TO RITA VADZINSKAYA

---

I opened my notebook and read.

*Nouns, verbs, declensions, conjugations*
*Hypotenuses and dictations,*
*When tests annoyed us past endurance*
*We took out anti-flunk insurance.*

Then there were a few lines about our Greek teacher, the
one who taught us Classical Greek syntax:

*The Greek came in, we all rose up*
*Like hairs upon a frightened head.*

And this was what I wrote about the class crybaby Zuzya
Kozelsky:

*He coughed whenever teachers wheezed,*
*He blew his nose when teachers sneezed.*
*He froze with fear (he was no hero)*
*Waiting for his grade of—zero.*
*He nagged ya, begged ya, teased ya, used ya,*
*Such a sniveler was our Zuzya!*

Then there was something about our school inspector Proshka:

> *A great detective, our inspector*
> *Loved to spy and watch and hector,*
> *Exercised his deep mentality*
> *To expose our criminality.*
> *The victim trapped, he pounced and chuckled,*
> *"AHA!—Your schoolbag isn't buckled."*
> *His wit was pointed as a spike:*
> *He always called a Jew a kike.*

And there was a lot more than that. Verses about Six-Eyes, Finti-Monti, Grishka Zuyev. There were a few lines about our Latin professor, Pavel Ilich Kavun.

That reminded me: today we—or rather, not "we" but "they"—were having the Latin lesson. My favorite subject. I would have given anything to be standing in front of that class, next to the teacher's lectern, chanting out loud:

> *Regia solis erat*
> *Sublimibus alta columnis.*

I would watch Pavel Ilich drinking in the ancient Roman words together with me. He would screw up his eyes and nod his head in rhythm.

I shivered. For the first time I understood my situation clearly. I would never stand in that schoolroom again.

The hell with everything that reminded me of the gymnasium! The hell with my *Gymnasiada!* What did it mean to me now? In a fury, I ripped my poor little manuscript to shreds. I tore it up into little pieces so that nobody would ever be able to read a single line of it. And then I climbed down from the Wigwam, ran over to the trash barrel, waved away the flies buzzing around it—and threw all my bits of paper into it.

Then I felt better, and I ran home by the back courts.

As soon as I walked into our room, Marusya motioned me to be silent. Mama had been suffering with a migraine headache since early morning. She was lying there not moving, her face dark with pain. Her head was wrapped up with a big towel, which Marusya dipped into a basin filled with vinegar every twenty minutes to freshen it.

"Mama went to the gymnasium," she said to me in a whisper heavy with accusation. 'She went there for *your* papers! The principal shouted at her. Yes, shouted. And all because of *you*, because of *you*!"

I stood by my mother's bed and then walked into the kitchen so as not to start bawling in front of her. Marusya handed me three five-kopeck coins.

"If I were you I would go to Gavrilenko's right away and buy some bread for supper and half a pound of pearl barley."

I took the money and wandered listlessly over to Gavrilenko's shop, on the corner of Old Portofrankovskaya Street. The first person I bumped into, before I even reached the corner, was Tuntin. He was the picture of self-satisfaction, carrying a heavy cane, although gymnasium students were strictly forbidden to carry sticks, umbrellas, canes and clubs. Tuntin hung around our neighborhood quite a bit because his aunt, the widow of some Moscow big shot, lived there and rented a whole floor from Madam Shershenevich.

Tuntin was the last person in the world I felt like seeing. But he looked as friendly as could be and gave me a big smile.

"Hi," he said. "Boy, do you look green and skinny! Six-Eyes came in today and did he ever curse you out! He said you were a black sheep. 'Thank the Lord he won't be in our gymnasium any more! The black sheep spoils the whole flock,' he said. Those were his exact words. 'Thank the Lord!' My mother says the same thing. You don't belong in a gymnasium, you belong in a laundry. After all, your mother—"

"You pig-face!" I screamed at him. That self-satisfied smirk of his was the mark of everything cruel and vicious that had been torturing me all these days. One single desire took hold of me: to scratch, bite, punch that arrogant face. The desire gave me ten times my normal strength, and to my own amazement I threw myself at the flabbergasted Tuntin, grabbed his cane away from him, broke it in half and threw it in his face.

I had performed what was to me a miracle. The cane was strong as steel, and normally I not only couldn't have broken it, I couldn't even have bent it.

I waited for Tuntin to start howling, to start using his big fists on me. But suddenly his face twisted in fright. And letting out a kind of squeal, he turned and ran through his aunt's gateway like the coward he was.

# 18

## I Become An Artist

A few more days went by. One day Top Hat showed up at our place, took me off in a corner and whispered, "Want to make some big money?" He gave me a wink and went through the motions of somebody sorting out a big bundle of bank notes.

I looked at him. Was he trying to drag me into some shady deal? But no—nothing of the kind. The sign painter, Anakhovich, needed a temporary handyman. And the question was, did I want the job for twenty kopecks a day, with eats on the house?

I was drunk with excitement. Anakhovich was no ordinary painter. He made all the best signs in town for tobacco shops, barbers, bars and laundries. Every sign was as high as a door, and he always printed in the lower right-hand corner: "Artist L. Anakhovich."

For tobacco shops, he would paint a fat Turk in a red fez, sitting on a divan and happily smoking Turkish tobacco out of a long hookah with a delicate stream of Turkish smoke spiraling out of it. And what didn't Anakhovich dream up for the barbers? Young men with magnificent moustaches, a comb resting behind their ears as they leaned over their clients in elegant poses, clicking their huge, silvery scissors.

In general, Anakhovich's signs and the work of other artisans like him made up the only art gallery in our town. Not long before, when another painter, Bendel, a rival of Anakhovich's, had painted a sign for the Northern Hotel showing four gentlemen with pinched-in waists, playing pool on an emerald-green table, the townspeople came running to get a look at this new work of art. It didn't bother them in the least that all the men looked as alike as drops of water, or that the arms holding the cues were twisted out of shape at the elbows.

Small wonder then that I was thrilled by Top Hat's proposition. I was sure that as soon as Anakhovich took one look at me he would hand over all his brushes and paints, and I would start right out painting those same magnificent Turks and look-alike gentlemen frozen over emerald-green pool tables.

But Anakhovich just looked at me and said in a bored voice, "There's a spatula over there in the corner. Be on the roof tomorrow morning. Sadovaya Street Number 8."

"What about the brushes?" I asked.

"The brushes, young man, will come in a year, maybe in two years."

I learned that a spatula was a long stick with a pointed scraper at its tip. And that before a roof could be painted, it had to be freed of all its rust and last year's paint, and be scraped down to the bare surface.

I became a roof scraper.

A scraper isn't the same thing as a spackler. A scraper does the crude work. He climbs up to the smoke-blackened, flaking roof, takes off his jacket, shirt and shoes, wraps his legs and feet with rags and, with the help of the spatula, he transforms the filthy, pockmarked roof into a spotless one. When he's done, the painters come and spackle the roof with plaster. And then they paint it crimson, green or even flaming yellow, so that the house looks suddenly young again and becomes an ornament to the street.

It was pleasantly cool in the mornings. A wind would be blowing in from the sea. But toward noon the southern spring sun would start baking the roof. I would go sit by the chimney for my break. Anakhovich's son, Boris Leopoldovich, who inspected all his father's jobs, soon appeared, carrying a basket. He'd stick his hand into it and come up with an onion, a hunk of bread, and a bottle of sourish kvass. That was what Anakhovich called "eats on the house."

I'd relax by the chimney for a half hour or so and then go back to work with my scraper again, and when I was finished I swept up the rubbish. I was pleased when there was a big pile of scrapings. That meant my work wasn't for nothing!

I came to like what I was doing. It was nice being outside all day long, looking down from a great height at the Tuntins and Fidos and Proshkas of the world, swarming down below like ants. It was nice seeing my work turn out well and knowing that on Saturday I'd be bringing home the ruble I had earned.

At the beginning, when I went home from work filthy, walking down the same streets which had so recently seen me as a gymnasium student with a silver crest on my cap, I had a feeling of terrible shame. So as not to show anybody that I felt like an outcast, I deliberately put an arrogant expression on my face. It was nothing but empty bravado, because I was hurting inside.

But little by little I got used to my situation. Finally I didn't even care any more when Madam Shershenevich, spotting me from her balcony, would turn her head away, pretending to be busy with her flowers or her dogs. She never yelled any more, "Hello there! Why are you stooped over like that? You're not seventy years old yet!"

But the bitter feelings took hold of me with new force the moment I caught a glimpse of my mother washing clothes or sewing. I'd start feeling sorry for myself and for her all over again. My mother, as always, kept silent. She even seemed pleased about my finding a job so fast. But she looked so pinched and shrunken that I wanted very much to make things up to her.

Finally, I came to a decision. I told my mother about it in confidence and asked her to keep it secret from Marusya. The plan was simple enough, but making it come true wasn't so easy.

"Mamochka, I'll do it all. Just you wait and see!"

My mother looked at me unbelievingly. Then something happened that I'll never forget. She suddenly pulled me toward her and kissed me on the cheeks, the neck, the chin, the eyes.

Such a thing had never happened in our family. As far back as I could remember, my mother never kissed either

Marusya or me. She was always very kind but very firm. Maybe it was the unexpectedness of that affectionate caress that shook me up so much. I jumped up and said with conviction, "I'll begin tomorrow. Just you wait and see!"

# 19

## I Go On with My Studies

After a while an important new occupation turned up to make my life more interesting. One morning I took a book to work with me. The first thing I did after climbing up my ladder to the roof was to pick up a piece of chalk and write on the roof in giant-sized English letters.

I LOOK. MY BOOK. I LOOK AT MY BOOK.

I wrote thirty or forty lines at a time and then walked back and forth on top of them, trying to learn them all by heart.

I studied the English language before beginning work every morning. I found a textbook at the flea market for twenty-five kopecks: *The English Language Self-Taught*, by Professor Meiendorf—a thick, tattered book with a number of pages missing, as I discovered later.

This Professor Meiendorf must have been a very

strange fellow. Every now and then he would ask his readers ridiculous questions like:

"Does the gardener's two-year-old son love the granddaughter of his daughter?"

"Do you have an aunt who buys bullfinches and canaries from the baker?"

But never mind. I would have been content to scribble over all my roofs with answers to these weird questions, because the professor guaranteed that every reader who paid the necessary attention to his canaries and aunts would learn the English language to perfection.

I believed the professor totally. Every day I wrote on my iron pages such ridiculous nonsense as:

"Does the mysterious stranger see the red tree of the farmer on which a blue cow is sitting and smiling?"

And even though I couldn't quite figure out whether the crazy cow was perched on the branches of the red tree or on the farmer's back, the fundamentals of English grammar became firmly rooted in me. I dreamed about the wonderful future day when Shakespeare and Walter Scott and my favorite of all, Charles Dickens, would become as understandable to me as Tolstoy, say, or Gogol. I'll never forget the wild happiness I felt when Ludwig Meier loaned me a book by the great American poet Edgar Allan Poe. I read a poem called "Annabel Lee," and discovered that I could understand almost every word of it. I decided that Annabel Lee was Rita Vadzinskaya, and I used to recite the poem out loud from the rooftops while I was working.

*It was many and many a year ago,*
*In a kingdom by the sea,*

# I Go On with My Studies

*That a maiden there lived whom you may know*
*By the name of Annabel Lee;—*
*And this maiden she lived with no other thought*
*Than to love and be loved by me.*

Of course, I didn't suspect that a real Englishman
would never guess he was listening to the English language. For Professor Meiendorf didn't teach me (how
could he?) how to pronounce the words.

It wasn't only English that I studied during this time.
I managed to find some textbooks and also a copy of the
sixth-year gymnasium curriculum at a secondhand book
stall, and started studying algebra, Latin and history at
night. Strangely enough, the gymnasium course was sur-
prisingly easy when I studied it without teachers and
supervisors, and in my own Wigwam instead of inside
school walls.

Timosha used to come to see me often, and the two of
us would study together. My studies were a great surprise
and pleasure for my mother. During the first month after
I was expelled she was sure my education was over, and
that the best thing I could hope for in life was to become
a clerk in some miserable little store.

But now, little by little, she began to realize that the
most cherished dream of her life, a dream she had thought
was smashed, was coming true in spite of all that had
happened. She would listen to Timosha and me going
over our work as if she were listening to music. The quan-
tities of purple eggplants, cherry dumplings, cantaloupes
and watermelons she treated Timosha to were beyond
counting. Again she began humming her marvelous songs
while she was bending over the washtub or watering her

plants. Again she would laugh till she cried at the antics of *Dead Souls* and *Pan Khalyavsky*. And as I watched her grow more lighthearted, I tried even harder to penetrate the mysteries of Krayevich's *Physics* and Kuner's *Latin Grammar*.

Even Simonenko the cop started to treat me better. One Sunday he was painting the fence around his front yard. I got my brushes and went to help him. Before long the whole fence was bright red. In a surge of gratitude he tried to shove a silver ruble into my hand. I refused to take it. That really touched him, and he asked me if I wanted a job at the local police precinct as assistant to the clerk.

"It's a good job, a nice fat job."

The clerks who worked at the police station were all crooks. And, since they took a payoff from people for every service they performed, they were all well off. They rode around in cabs, wore fancy neckties, smoked cigars and got drunk.

Simonenko himself held down an easy and profitable job. Every morning he would put on his stained policeman's tunic and go over to Market Square to make sure the peddlers weren't cheating the customers by palming off stale vegetables and rotten fish, or by tipping their scales, or selling wormy meat, or wine without a license.

You might think the merchants would start shivering when Simonenko showed up. But they greeted him like a long-lost friend. He would walk past their stands with a big smile on his face, as if he was there to congratulate them on the weather. His hefty maid, Maria, walked behind him. Cheerfully, the merchants would load her huge market basket with fish, lard, grain, hams, olives, nuts and the choicest fruits. And they never asked for a penny.

All this was because Simonenko was so "bighearted." He willingly allowed these peddlers to palm off all kinds of stale, flyblown merchandise and rotten goods on their customers. He never checked on their false scales and never fined them for the unsanitary condition of their stalls.

This was done right out in the open. No one ever called Simonenko a chiseler or a bribe taker. Just the opposite. Everybody said he was a good fellow. All the tenants in our house (except my mother and Marusya) respected and praised him. Anytime a housewife needed the loan of an iron, or a mortar and pestle, or sieve, or coffee grinder, she would go to Simonenko.

He gave charity to beggars and monks. On holidays he prayed regularly at the Kasperov Church of the Sisters of Charity on the corner of Old Portofrankovskaya Street.

And I distinctly remember a big round piece of jellied fruit candy he gave me once when I was six years old. I was standing in the courtyard, crying. Simonenko came out of his front yard and popped a fruit candy into my mouth. It smelled of tobacco and herring, but it dried up my tears right away.

The cops in our town were so corrupt, such bullies and toughs, that next to them the "bighearted" chiseler Simonenko seemed like a righteous man.

# 20

## Creep

---

After that things took a turn for the worse. Anakhovich had less and less work. The painting season had come to an end. He then fixed me up with a job pasting up posters. Dozens of fast-running young boys worked in the group, each one going off to a different neighborhood. I was assigned to a very distant location. I too ran down alleys and streets with a brush and a bucket of paste, hastily pasting up posters on walls, fences and the announcement posts on street corners.

---

ZEVEKE'S FAMOUS MENAGERIE IS HERE

---

Ai, How Lovely in Isakovich's Swimming Pool!

---

CAPTAIN DE VETRIO!!
The Man with the Iron Stomach!
Swallows Broken Bottles and Glasses!!
Also Frogs and Snakes!!!!

---

## VENTRILOQUIST
# P A N T A L E I M O N   V A N Y U K H I N
### and His Talking Dolls

---

## Utochkin! *Utochkin!!* U T O C H K I N ! ! !

The work was more than I could manage. It would have been easier for two people working together, but doing it alone was clumsy and hard. I lasted a week. Through a recommendation from Simonenko I started giving private lessons to a middle-aged military clerk who needed to master the fourth-year gymnasium curriculum in order to get a promotion. This clerk, who at first seemed like a timid, pleasant fellow, turned out to be a terrible skinflint. He never paid me the two and a half rubles he promised me.

Then I fell into a different line of work. Every evening I would read novels printed in the magazines *Rodina* and *Niva* to an elderly colonel's widow. While I was still on page one she would fall asleep and start to snore. As my reading was coming to an end the old lady would give herself a shake, pretend that she had been wide awake the whole time and shower me with praise. And she paid me a silver ruble for every visit.

This job had been found for me by Lida Kuryndina. Lida treated me with friendly concern, as ever. She dug up five or six textbooks which I needed as much as I needed bread to eat, and for Easter she gave me a present of an English dictionary. And how many cold cutlets she carried to the library that I ran to on Sundays, after studying with Timosha and Munya!

"They gave me cutlets again," she would say, screwing up her nose and making a funny face. "I can't stand cutlets. Please eat them or else I'll have to throw them away!"

The cutlets were peppery, dry and hard, but I ate them with great relish. In the first place I had to save poor Lida from eating them. In the second place, I developed a bottomless hunger at that time, probably because I had grown so much in the past few months.

One day that summer when I was still scraping roofs and was on my way home after work, I saw Rita Vadzinskaya from a distance. A wild happiness poured over me like scalding water—the same feeling I always got when I caught a glimpse of her on the street.

> For the moon never beams without bringing me
>    dreams
>   Of the beautiful Annabel Lee;
> And the stars never rise but I see the bright eyes
>   Of the beautiful Annabel Lee . . .

She was standing with her girl friend near an ice-cream vendor's tub. The vendor was digging out the frozen gold ice-cream balls from his tub, wrapped in dirty white canvas. As I passed, I felt a surge of love and bashfulness that made me stoop even more than usual.

I hadn't walked more than two steps past her when Rita said, "God, what a creep!"

Her girl friend laughed and started chanting, "Once he worked with books and paper, now he's just an old roof scraper!"

I was stunned. I couldn't believe my ears. *Creep!* Is there an uglier, more vulgar word than that? And this was the girl I called my "Annabel Lee," the girl I once dedicated my poem *Gymnasiada* to! The words of a different poem suddenly crept into my mind.

> *Why didn't I see it before?*
> *She isn't worth loving,*
> *She isn't worth hating,*
> *She isn't worth mentioning.*

Strangely, by the time I turned down my own street my pain was evaporated and replaced by a feeling of happiness. It was like breaking out of the net my hands and feet were tangled up in. Best of all was that now I was free to fall in love with Lida Kuryndina. Now *there* was a girl who would never have a repulsive word like "creep" in her vocabulary!

# 21

## Everything Falls to Pieces

That didn't mean that everything in my life was smooth and easy from then on. Nothing of the kind. Inside of a year my worst enemy turned up and almost managed to crush me.

That enemy was—myself.

I studied very hard at first and mastered the whole store of sixth-year knowledge by diligent work. But the year after that, instead of applying the same stubborn determination to the seventh-year curriculum, I was overcome by inertia.

I threw my textbooks aside, fought with Timosha and just couldn't seem to pull myself together. Finally I became an out-and-out loafer.

It all began very innocently.

I was an ardent fan of Utochkin, who hadn't yet become a famous flyer. How could he? Airplanes did not exist yet. He was a young man just at the start of his career as a champion bike racer. There wasn't another racer in the world—not a Russian, not a foreigner—who could beat him in our city cyclodrome.

If anyone had told me then that there were heroes more deserving of honor than Utochkin, I would have taken such a remark as an insult. For hours on end, we boys sat on the fence around the cyclodrome in the broiling sun, just to see Utochkin—maybe at the thirtieth turn—glue himself to the bike handle and suddenly shoot out in front like a whirlwind, leaving his competitors behind. The crowds would scream like mad, as thrilled by Utochkin's victory as if it was their own.

My pals Munya and Timosha were crazy about Utochkin too. But their excitement never reached the hysterical point mine did. I gave my soul to Utochkin. My real thrill came once when I saw him in Sarafonov's Delicatessen, where he was buying sausage and wine just like an ordinary person.

Noticing my hypnotized stare, he stretched out his hand and ruffled my hair with his stubby reddish fingers. That was a big event in my life. I bragged about it for weeks.

Everything would have been all right if that was my only infatuation. But no. I took to kite flying with the same mania. Once more, my old dream took hold of me— to construct such a fantastic kite that it could grapple with Vaska Pechonkin's kite and conquer it in an air battle.

Through great effort I managed to get my hands on some top-quality towline, the kind we used to call "English twine," and a huge sheet of pale-blue draftsman's paper. I took all these treasures over to Vanya Aligeraki, my partner and co-builder.

"That's going to be some super-kite, oho-ho! Let's give it a name, 'Death to the Pechonkies.'"

It was the beginning of my big sellout. Every morning, instead of sitting down to my books, I would go over to Vanya's hideout. Vanya would be sitting on the floor in a pile of trash, completely absorbed in building the kite. "Good thing you came to lend a hand!" he would say when he saw me.

But he didn't really want my help at all. He needed me only as a respectful witness, so he could show off and act important.

No matter what he was doing—building the bamboo frame, measuring the guide ropes or tying the knots in the tail, he was greedy for approval and praise. If I forgot to praise him he would praise himself. He had such a good opinion of himself that gradually I started to believe he couldn't make a mistake. When people are very sure of themselves other people seem to believe in them too. At least it's always been like that with me.

"What an eye I have—it's as good as a compass!" What glue I made—you could glue iron with it!"

And when I asked him about the tail, which he had put together out of scraps of fabric and tape, he assured me that it was a wonderful tail, a fantastically strong tail, knotted together firmly with his own two hands.

In three or four days the kite was ready. A giant super-kite, as big as a bull calf. I painted an ugly goggle-eyed face on it with ocher and red lead paint, and underneath I printed in gigantic letters: DEATH TO THE PECHONKIES!

Then we rewound the whole length of twine on a long oak block, in a figure eight. We hid the kite behind the troughs under the ox shed and waited for a good strong wind to lift it up into the sky where it could go into battle with Pechonkin's kite.

All week it was deadly calm. Finally, on Sunday, a wind came up. The laundry hanging on the line began jerking and flapping. Dust flew down the streets, and the girls passing our gate squealed and held their skirts close to their knees.

The time had come. I climbed up to the roof with the kite. Down below, Vanya stood motionless for a long time. Suddenly he shouted up to me, "NOW!" threw the twine block on the ground, let the cord pass through his left fist and ran with it toward the gate.

The kite slapped me in the face and then slowly lifted up over the houses, where it was seized by a puff of wind and carried aloft. Happy, excited, I jumped down and grabbed the cord away from Vanya.

It seemed to me that the kite was as happy as we were. Gaily flapping its long tail, it didn't fuss or fidget around but soared calmly up. Now everyone for blocks around could see what a beauty and a powerhouse we had! All the boys wanted to hold the cord "for a second," but Vanya bellowed so loud they stopped asking.

But where was Pechonkin? Surely he must have seen our giant and realized that tangling with it was beyond his power. I pictured him, sore and sullen, together with the rest of the Pechonkies.

An hour went by. Suddenly, from behind the low stable of a neighboring house, Pechonkin's kite floated up, looking almost timid, even bashful. How plain and small it seemed! What use was it, that pitiful little baby? Our twine was a thousand times stronger than Pechonkin's.

Just let him start up with us, and that would be the end of him!

We were shouting "Hooray!" and celebrating our victory in advance when Pechonkin's shabby kite tried to approach ours. And then something incredible happened. Our calm, proud, mighty giant started swooping around. It made an enormous zigzag in the sky, plunged down as if it had been shot through the heart and disappeared in some faraway street, tree or rooftop, leaving us holding a useless piece of string.

Vanya let out a yell and sat down on the ground.

"You, you . . . it's all your fault!" I shouted at him.

I started pummeling him with my fists. We rolled around in the dirt. He writhed, bit my hands, sank his nails into my ear and howled. From behind the wall we could hear the Pechonkies gloating in their joy.

What I had said was true. It was Vanya's fault. The tail, that fantastically strong tail he had been bragging about, so firmly knotted together, was worthless because the material between the knots, the tapes and scraps of fabric, were rotted.

In the end Pechonkin was smarter than we were. Realizing that he could never snap the cord of our super-kite, he took a different approach. He simply tore off our rotten tail with one powerful tug of his own kite. And a kite without a tail is no better than a stone.

If we had had any sense, we would have tried to save the cord by gathering up the undamaged part of it as soon as the disaster occurred; and then we should have run straight to the place where the kite had fallen. Instead, Vanya and I knocked each other around in a fit of spite— to the satisfaction of the Pechonkies, who instantly ran to

where our precious English twine was lying and tore it
to bits.

That evening I dragged my way home miserable and
bedraggled, covered with bruises and with a rip in my
jacket. I felt ashamed, sitting at the table next to my
mother, eating her kasha, her brynza cheese, her borshch,
her bread. Marusya kept glaring at me, and I spent a
sleepless night.

Every night after that I saw the senselessness and stu-
pidity of what I was doing. I called myself all kinds of
names—a parasite, a drone, a vicious embezzler of my own
best years—and I promised myself that I would straighten
myself out. But then morning would come and again
something would pull me outside, either to the steamships
and sailboats in the harbor, or to the bike races, or to a
fire or a cockfight, or just to chase Simonenko's pigeons
around. Anything to keep from laying a finger on a
textbook.

All this time my mother never so much as threw an
angry look my way. But her lips would tremble and press
together as soon as I walked in the door.

One day, as I was walking down Novorybnaya Street,
I saw Father Melety. Handsome, imposing, he responded
so benignly to the bows of the passersby! I shied away from
him like a wild buffalo. I couldn't let the man who had
destroyed me see what a pitiful savage I had become, and
take pleasure in my misery.

This binge of loafing lasted for some months. It turned
into a deadly bore, drifting around from morning to night
searching for amusements. I came to realize that doing
nothing is more than a disgrace—it's a torment.

But I didn't show this to anybody. Just the opposite. I flaunted my recklessness in everybody's face. I can still see the look of horror on Lida Kuryndina when, in answer to her reproaches about my behavior, I amazed myself by letting loose a stream of curse words.

The other tenants in our house began keeping their distance from me. Motya, the draymen's cook, would say every time she bumped into me, "Bad business when a kid doesn't have a father! You wouldn't be turning into such riffraff if you had your Papasha at home."

That July I left home altogether and stopped seeing my mother and Marusya. I said some sickeningly nasty things to my mother and announced that I was leaving forever. Uncombed, bareheaded, in my torn, rusty shoes, very skinny and very hungry, I took to loitering around the dusty city, doing nothing.

The Pechonkies became my only companions. I hung around with them for hours, fishing, hunting for tarantulas, playing pitch and toss. If I won a couple of kopecks, I would buy myself a piece of bread and a glass of kvass.

It was a lucky thing for me that Malanka, who used to help my mother out with the laundry, was living with her husband Savelly in a dark basement room on Great Arnautskaya Street. When I got so hungry I couldn't stand it, I would go down the crooked steps to Malanka's basement, and she would give me something to eat—sometimes a tomato, sometimes cornmeal mush, sometimes a piece of fish. Later she told me that all this food—including my favorite cherry dumplings—had been given to her in secret by my mother, to feed me with.

I slept on the beach in a big scow that belonged to the old fisherman Semmelidi. But word of this hideout got around, and soon some other homeless boys took it over. They threw rocks and lumps of clay at me and drove me away. There was nothing left to do but sleep on the bare sand, which became unbearably cold by morning.

I don't know what would have become of me if that aimless life had gone on till winter. I would doubtless have become a tramp and frozen to death somewhere in the steppe under the snow.

# 22

## Life Begins Again

S trange at it seems, I was saved by the flu. Our town was the first to be hit by the epidemic. The doctors didn't know how to treat it at that time, and many people died of it.

Poor Timosha caught it too. He was in bed for a long time and fell far behind the class. But Trustee of the Educational District von Lustig, as a special favor, gave him permission to take a makeup exam in the fall.

I didn't know about any of this directly. It was months since I had seen any of my old school friends. But one day I ran into Timosha's sister, "two-toned Liza," at the port on New Jetty, where I was sitting with one of the Pechonkin gang, trying to catch a bullhead for my supper. She flew at me like a whirlwind and demanded that I go with her right away to visit Timosha, because he was sick and lonesome and missed me.

Roughly, I pretended I wasn't interested. But by the

next morning I wanted to see him so badly that I cleaned up my shoes, smoothed down my hair and went down the old familiar road to the house that looked like a ship.

There was the sea—calm, pale lilac-colored, as if the sun had faded it. The seagulls circled overhead endlessly. And up above the narrow ship's staircase on the "deck" was Timosha himself, skinny and weak-looking, surrounded by books and notes and medicine bottles.

When he saw me he got so excited he couldn't say a word. I sat there, all ruffled up, and also kept silent. Finally he managed to get out a word about the seagulls—how repulsive they were, how greedy. He stuttered worse than ever. I realized then that he was ashamed of his weakness and his stuttering. That made me feel good. I'd been thinking that he would look down on me with insulting pity, the way everybody else did. And now it seemed that he was envying me and could use a little pity himself.

As soon as I understood this, I felt really sorry for him. And when he showed me his algebra problem, which he couldn't solve, I tried to show off my knowledge. To my own amazement, I solved the problem. He showed me another problem, a tricky one, about two moving trains. For a long time we tried to work it out together, and finally I solved it. Then we translated a passage from Vergil's *Aeneid*. Somehow, after I left Timosha, I didn't go to the Pechonkin gang or the cyclodrome or the funeral of General Podushkin. Instead, I climbed up to my loft and dragged out the textbooks which had been lying around my Wigwam so long.

The friendliest meeting of all was with Professor Meiendorf's *English Language Self-Taught*. I could have kissed that book. I felt a surge of happiness at reading about blue cows sitting on red trees and aunts who bought their canaries and bullfinches at the bakery. To this day I am grateful to that odd character Professor Meiendorf. If not for him, I would never have been able to read Shakespeare or William Blake or Coleridge or Shelley in the original, or those other great English poets I came to love.

The next morning at long last, guilty and sheepish, I went back to our own apartment.

My mother was standing and ironing. I was positive she would greet me with a hail of accusations and that I would have to break down and cry in front of her and swear to make up for everything. But she just looked at me with her familiar calm friendliness, as if I had never been away, and said in the most normal voice—with just a trace of shakiness in it—"The borshch is in the oven and the bagels are on the table under a napkin."

Marusya, who was sitting bent over a book, measured me with her annihilating glare, and was obviously on the point of making some biting remark. But she too kept herself under control and merely said, "If I were you I would go and get a haircut."

And then she buried herself in her book again.

From that day on I got down to work. Every morning I would leave the house with a tremendous sausage or bacon sandwich and eat it while walking to Timosha's house to master physics, Latin and Classical Greek together with him. Since Timosha and I were used to studying together, we quickly got ourselves organized. And soon a hope was born in me—the hope that I could carry out the promise I swore to my mother on that moonlight night a year before. Later, when I went back to my own place in the loft, I felt that nothing could ever tempt me away again from the straight path. My diabolical obsession was over and done with, and I would never give in to it again.

# 23

## An Amazing Event

During those miserable months after I left home and began leading my senseless street life, I had stopped reading almost altogether. Now, I fell on my books greedily. I went straight through the English writers—Charles Dickens, Samuel Smiles, Herbert Spencer, Henry Thomas Buckle, and read the complete works of the Russian authors Leskov and Turgenev. But what really excited me was the writing of the radical critic Pisarev, whose works Finti-Monti had given me some time ago with the caution, "Mind now—don't you show them to anybody!"

Reading books like these at white heat, I felt myself transformed into a "critical thinker." Out of the clear blue sky I announced one day to my sister Marusya that from now on I considered dancing, music and the other arts "pernicious" because, I insisted, they "impede mankind on its thorny path to social justice."

Marusya responded by calling me a "pitiful vandal,"

but I could tell by her tone of voice that she secretly admired me. The truth was, she found it pleasant to have a brother who was capable of throwing around phrases like "thorny path," "social justice" and "mankind" and who knew what a "vandal" was.

As a matter of fact, I didn't hold my firm point of view for long. Before the month was out I was prancing through the quadrille and the polka to the music of violins, flutes and bassoons at the wedding of Celia and Top Hat—forgetting that by doing so I was "impeding mankind on its thorny path to social justice."

Timosha recovered from his illness so completely that by the end of September, after passing all his makeup exams, he started going out with me in his father's Customs launch, the *Typhoon*. He wasn't able to row as yet— he was still too feeble for that—but he sat back in the stern and gave the orders. The rowers were his sister, "two-toned Liza," and me.

Once we took along Lida Kuryndina, who was deathly afraid of sea voyages. I doubt whether she got much fun out of that excursion. The normally polite Timosha became an unforgivable boor on the water. When Lida innocently used the word "seat" he pretended he didn't understand what she was talking about. In a boat you weren't supposed to call a seat a seat, you had to call it a "thwart." And a couple of minutes later, when I dared to refer to his little craft as a "boat," he said indignantly, "There is no such thing as a 'boat.' For a sailor there's a dinghy, or a launch, or a scow, or a punt or a skiff. But the word 'boat'—that's something L-l-lida made up herself."

He kept that up all afternoon. But as soon as our trip

was over and we stepped up on the Customs dock, he changed back into the old Timosha.

Soon Lida Kuryndina and I became real friends again. She found me an excellent job for the fall. I was to tutor two quick, bright boys in Latin. Their father, Vartan, was a Moldavian, an usher in the Municipal Theater. Not only did he pay me well—twelve rubles a month—he also let me go up to the balcony for free. It was there that I first heard *Carmen* (performed by the famous Figner Touring Company), *The Queen of Spades, The Huguenots* and *Eugene Onegin.*

Around that time my affairs took a turn for the better. My Uncle Foma came to visit us and made me a present of his own Ukrainian peasant sheepskin coat. Naturally it wasn't new, it was even patched, but that gave it a special charm. I managed to pick up a shaggy cap at the flea market. This outfit made me feel terrific.

Spring came, then summer. Our life grew smoother, little by little.

And then something happened which struck me like thunder. It all began when Madam Shershenevich, walking her dogs past our house, shouted to me from some distance away, "Hello!"

I was surprised at this, since she had stopped greeting me long ago.

"Hello—hello there!" she repeated, with a glint in her eye. "That Top Hat of yours—what do they call him now? Stock, or is it Stoss? What an 'artist' he turned out to be! Just imagine! But I always said, I always—"

"Yuzya Stock? What's the matter with him?" I asked.

"As if you didn't know!" she laughed. "Isn't he supposed to be your best friend? You should know better than anybody!"

Still laughing, she walked away.

I began to worry. What was she so happy about? What had happened to Top Hat? I hadn't seen him for a long time.

He lived on Great Arnautskaya Street, in the same building where Malanka was now living. I ran over to see him. His courtyard was packed to the rafters with tenants. That wasn't unusual in our town. Tenants never stayed in their own rooms, but hung around their oil stoves, frying pans and washtubs right outside in the courtyard. They fried their mackerel in sunflower oil there, and poured out their dirty slops without stepping away from their own doorsteps. They fought, they cursed at each other and then made up again. And all day long, from morning to night, they shouted at their numberless children, who shouted back at them.

An outsider might think, seeing a crowd in a courtyard, that some catastrophe had taken place, that a house had collapsed, or somebody had been stabbed. But it was only an ordinary courtyard packed with people from the south of Russia, people who were incapable of doing anything quietly. The courtyard quieted down only in June or July, when the sun started baking it. Then the entire court population, to rescue itself from the sun's merciless rays, would retreat behind closed shutters into tiny, airless rooms and snore peacefully to the accompaniment of buzzing flies.

But as soon as the first shadow of twilight made its appearance in the courtyard, the windows flew open, people ran into the yard and the same noisy life started up and would not stop again till late at night, when the magnificent southern stars filled the sky.

Making my way through the court was like trying to work through a military formation. Dozens of curious eyes followed me. I went up to a woman who was bending over a half-reclining neighbor and searching her head for insects in a businesslike way.

"Where does Yuzya Stock live? Top Hat, I mean . . ."

As soon as I mentioned that name, the woman looked up and called over to a bald-headed fellow, "He's asking for Stock-Top Hat!" She shouted this out in a happy, ringing voice, as if she was telling him some very funny joke.

The bald-headed fellow looked at me in amazement. Turning to an old lady in a bathrobe, he pointed me out to her.

"He's asking for Stock-Top Hat!"

They both burst out laughing. And the whole courtyard laughed with them.

# 24

## Where is the Truth?

People came running toward us from every part of the court—young ones, old ones and a whole gang of kids. They looked me over curiously. Finally one of them, holding a yardstick in his hand—a tailor, evidently—said with exaggerated politeness, "You are looking for Top Hat-Stock? If you are so interested to have his address, please, I can tell it to you."

And he winked at somebody in the crowd. "Kindly take a pencil and write it down. Kulikovo Field, City Jail, Cell Number . . . well, you'll find that out when you get there."

There was a new explosion of laughter.

Top Hat in jail? What kind of nonsense was that? I pushed through the thick crowd blocking my way and went down to Malanka's room, in the basement. It was a basement in name only. Actually it was a cellar without windows. A dim, stinking kerosene lamp burned in it day and night. The room was so damp that bread brought in from the bakery would get heavy and wet in two or three hours, as if it had been soaking in water.

Malanka told me what had happened. My beloved Top Hat, regarded by Mama and me and everybody else living in our house, even by Simonenko the cop, as such an honest, such an honorable man, a man we all believed when he told us he had long ago thrown over his old criminal "profession"—had turned out to be a thief! A week ago, he had broken into Madam Chikuanova's vacant apartment and cleaned it out. He took away her most precious possessions: a little casket filled with valuables, silver spoons, gold watches, even her little granddaughter's umbrella, brought from Japan.

"Lies," I said. "All lies. I'll never believe that Top Hat—I mean Yuzya—"

Savelly, Malanka's husband, a sullen, clumsy loafer, lifted himself up from the couch. People used to say that he hadn't taken off his hat or his boots in years. I never could understand how Malanka, with her soft voice and sweet smile, could have married a monster like him.

"Lies?" said Savelly, and advanced toward me threateningly. "Are you calling me a liar?"

It seems he had been a witness, an official witness for the police, when they searched Top Hat's room. Savelly had seen with his own eyes how Madam Chikuanova's casket, comb, handkerchiefs and granddaughter's Japanese umbrella were discovered under Top Hat's floorboards. Top Hat had sworn up and down that he had no idea where the articles came from. But the moment Madam Chikuanova saw them, she screamed out loud that all these things were hers, that they had been stolen from her apartment.

So that was the way things were! So Top Hat had been fooling us all, playing the part of a simple fellow. But he was still the same thief he had been four years ago, when my mother caught him in the act. And we believed in him as our dearest friend, believed he had changed under our influence!

And Celia! She believed in him, too. Poor Celia! She didn't let him take so much as a needle or a box of matches from anybody without asking permission. How she must be suffering now.

My mouth dried up. My legs felt so weak I had to sit down. Savelly went on talking. "And they carted Celia off to jail, too. What do you mean, 'why?' She's his wife, isn't she? They'll knock those gold watches out of her, believe you me. They'll clip her sharp nails for her."

It seems that when the cops carried out their search and asked Celia where she had stashed the watches stolen by Top Hat, she fell into such a furious rage that she started to scratch, bite and scream.

"She bit Karabash, the inspector of police . . . Anton Ignatievich. And you know those fists of his, oho-ho!"

I don't remember how I got out of that dismal cellar or made my way home to our own Rybnaya Street. Now— to see Simonenko, on the double! He'd know all about it. He was a cop, after all, he'd have to know.

Luckily, he was at home in his own front yard, sitting under a mulberry tree—gray-haired, good-humored and wearing an embroidered Ukrainian shirt. He was having a sip of cherry brandy and lazily brushing away the wasps. His brass trumpet lay on the table in front of him.

"Why are you so out of breath?" he asked.

"I have to talk over some business with you. Very important."

"Business? So—sit down and tell me. Did you decide to go in for police clerking?"

"No! It's something else . . . I want . . ."

"One minute!" And, without turning his head, he shouted loudly through the open window into the kitchen, "Glass!"

The maid Maria brought a glass and set it down in front of me with a bang. But it nauseated me even to think of sugary sweet cherry brandy.

"Drink. It's cold! Or maybe some beer?"

But I pushed the glass away. Only then did I notice that my hands were shaking.

"Top Hat," I started to stammer. "You know him— Yuzya Stock—"

Simonenko's eyes got big and round. "Rotten thief!" he yelled. "Faker! Doesn't want to live by honest work. Goes crawling around after other people's property."

I stared at him in amazement. This chiseler here, this fleecer who didn't have one piece of bread or lump of sugar in his whole house that he earned by "honest work," was yelling about a rotten thief who crawled around after other people's property. And his hatred was so sincere!

Simonenko calmed down and spoke in his normal voice. "Let me advise you as a friend. Don't get mixed up in this dirty business. I'm telling you this because I'm fond of you. It's straight from the heart. I wouldn't want them to drag you into it. Everybody knows that you and that— whatzisname?—Top Hat—are friends. Pals. Once they pull you into it you'll never get out. Particularly since

you're an illegitimate . . . because you don't have any papa
to take your part . . ."

I ran out to the street without even saying goodbye, and
immediately heard the sickening sounds of Simonenko's
trumpet in back of me. I hurried off to my two students—
I was late for the lesson already.

I talked to myself all the way there. Could it be that the
pair of them—Top Hat and Celia too—were such terrific
actors that they could have kept up appearances all these
years—played the part of honest people? Would Celia
have gone on working in that Gluzman and Romm candy
factory from early morning to late at night, for pennies a
day, if her husband was really a burglar who could always
pick up gorgeous dresses and gold watches for her?

# 25

## The Trial

I didn't get home till supper. My mother had already heard from Malanka that Top Hat and his wife were arrested.

"Would you believe it, what a slippery pair they were?" I said, sitting down at the kitchen table. "Making themselves out to be such goody-goodies. And we—fools that we were—we believed them."

My mother didn't answer for a few seconds, and then she said slowly, as if she was weighing out every word, "You can think what you want, but I'm still the same fool. I believe both of them are innocent—Top Hat and Celia too."

"How strange you are!" said Marusya in her cool, logical voice, which left no room for argument. "Think for yourself. How could they find an umbrella in *your* house, for example, and a jewel case, and the rest of Madam

Chikuanova's things—if you didn't snitch them in the first place? That's *absolutely* firsthand evidence."

"I don't know what you mean by *absolutely*," said my mother, just as deliberately as before. "But I do know Top Hat is no thief."

But the judge before whom Celia and Top Hat had to appear a few weeks later held a different opinion. He was unshakably convinced that a pair of thieves were standing before him. Top Hat had no luck at all trying to prove that he and Celia were at Celia's aunt's name-day party the night Madam Chikuanova's apartment was robbed, and that they had spent the night with the aunt. The judge sneered contemptuously and ordered the defendants to stop trying to obstruct justice and tell the court without any more beating around the bush exactly where they had stashed Madam Chikuanova's gold, diamonds, silver and china, valued at three thousand three hundred rubles.

In answer to this Celia said in a muffled voice, "Kill me, cut me to pieces, but . . . I never . . ." And she cried. (Later, I found out that she had been beaten up at the police station.)

Top Hat, with lifeless eyes and an exhausted look on his face, kept saying over and over in a monotone that he had never laid eyes on any umbrella or watch or jewel casket. But after years of sitting on the bench, the judge had stopped believing statements of that kind, since all thieves insist they're innocent when they're in court standing trial.

It looked as if the judge was in a big hurry to go somewhere. He kept looking at his watch every few minutes and barking at every witness, "All right, make it short, make it short!"

There was only one witness he listened to attentively— George Drakondidi, Zhorka, the fellow we all thought of as a deaf-mute. He had put on some weight and was wearing an expensive suit. Zhorka Drakondidi testified to the court that the defendant had once robbed the stall of the merchant Korytnikov at the market, at another time burglarized the country house of Titular Councilor Ehrlich's widow, and also stolen all the linen out of Hereditary Honorable Citizen Pantyushkin's attic.

The judge heard this witness out to the end. He looked at his watch again and got up to pronounce sentence. But just then the judge's secretary, a young man with a university pin in his lapel, approached the judge and began whispering something and showing the judge a folder with documents in it.

The judge scowled. But the secretary whispered even harder and drew a large document out of the folder. After that the judge, not bothering to hide his annoyance, ordered the guards to take the prisoner away, since the case of Yosif Stock and his wife Cecilia Stock was subject to further investigation.

I rushed over to Rybnaya Street to tell my mother about the goings-on in court that day. But she had one of her migraine headaches. She was lying on the couch with her face all yellowish. Marusya made a sign to me—"Go away"—and I left on tiptoe. When my mother had a migraine every sound made the pain worse.

A few days later, the whole situation changed. Zhorka Drakondidi (still dressed in his expensive suit) was arrested on Deribasovskaya Street in the Junkers Banking

Office, where he was trying to change some forged hundred-ruble notes. His apartment was searched, and nothing incriminating was found. But that night the police made a surprise raid on his brother Themistocles' Artificial Mineral Waters Establishment. And they uncovered a whole storehouse of valuables—gold earrings, rings . . . and, among other things, Madam Chikuanova's gold watch.

Then the real story came out. Zhorka was a professional burglar and his brother Themistocles, the soda water and syrup dealer, was a fence, a cover man. Besides Madam Chikuanova's watch the police found her late husband's medals, his gilt and diamond cigarette case and her ivory fan.

But then how could Madam Chikuanova's things turn up inside Top Hat and Celia's shack on Great Arnautskaya Street?

Three or four steps leading up to that shack were made of rotted boards. When the top step was lifted, it revealed a hollow leading to a cellar. And that was what Zhorka Drakondidi took advantage of. After he broke into Madam Chikuanova's apartment he kept the most valuable things for himself. But the other stuff—the jewel casket, the umbrella and the rest of the petty loot—he planted in Top Hat's shack, on a hot day when the tenants were all hiding from the sun behind their tight-closed shutters.

And then he wrote an anonymous letter to the Inspector of Police Karabash, stating that the stolen goods were hidden under the floorboards of such-and-such an apartment occupied by Yosif Stock, who had robbed Madam Chikuanova's apartment.

But why did Zhorka need to frame Top Hat? There

was a very simple reason for that. Practically from the age of twelve, Top Hat had been a member of Zhorka's gang, the leader of which was Themistocles Drakondidi. Top Hat worked for Drakondidi for several "seasons" before he decided to go straight.

Themistocles was furious. He had no doubt that sooner or later Top Hat would go to the cops and inform on him. For a long time, he tried to talk Top Hat into coming back to the stealing profession, luring him on with all kinds of big money talk. But Top Hat wasn't taken in.

Drakondidi wasn't afraid of the local police, because Inspector Karabash already knew what went on behind the scenes at the Artificial Mineral Waters Establishment. He was quite willing to make himself "blind" in exchange for the big cut he got from Drakondidi every month. The whole local police precinct was on Drakondidi's payroll, and therefore they looked the other way when he pulled off his deals.

But Inspector Karabash had no power outside his own precinct. He himself was under the jurisdiction of the City Chief of Police.

Drakondidi and his gang then decided to render Top Hat harmless and to get revenge on him at the same time. They planted the stolen goods on him.

There's no doubt that Top Hat would have been a goner if it hadn't been for one witness. The student Iglitsky, who lived in Top Hat's apartment house on the second floor, across the court from Top Hat's shack, was sitting by his window, playing chess with Ludwig Meier, when he happened to look out into the court. He saw the so-called "plumber" Zhorka pottering around near the rotted steps of Top Hat's shack.

## The Trial

At first Iglitsky paid no special attention to this. But later, when Top Hat was arrested, he remembered Zhorka's behavior and came forward with his strange evidence. And a new trial was set.

During the second trial Zhorka behaved with barefaced insolence, denying any connection with the case. Nevertheless the new judge pronounced him guilty, not only of burglarizing Madam Chikuanova's apartment, but also of a criminal attempt to make other people, honest people, shoulder the blame for his own crime.

There were quite a few university students in court, brought there by Iglitsky. Celia's friends were there too, and a lot of other young people. When Top Hat and Celia were acquitted, the whole courtroom went wild. They surrounded the defendants and began congratulating them, hugging them, kissing them.

I stood there alone, apart from everybody. I couldn't bring myself to go up to my old friends. I was ashamed to look them in the face. How could I have let myself be taken in by their enemies' lies, by the stories Malanka's husband Savelly had told me, and by the "bighearted" chiseler Simonenko?

Celia and Top Hat went home, worn out but happy. The whole courtyard on Great Arnautskaya Street met them with shouts of joy. When they went inside their little shack their neighbors followed after them, talking at the top of their voices and carrying enough tomatoes, eggplants and hard-boiled eggs to last for weeks (that is, if they hadn't held a celebration banquet at which all these goodies were gobbled up that night).

They borrowed chairs and knocked a table together out of some crates. The red-nosed tailor and his sprightly little

spouse (those were his exact words: "my spouse") con-
tributed a whole mountain of dried fish. Celia's mother
brought raisins, nuts and halvah. Bottles of beer turned up
from somewhere, and the guests sitting around the table
began congratulating Top Hat and assuring him that they
had all believed in his innocence from the first.

The guest of honor at this banquet was the student
Iglitsky. Every time a new guest arrived, he went into the
court and lifted up the rotten step to reveal the famous
hole through which Zhorka had planted Madam Chikuanova's things on Top Hat.

After that, the guests went over to Celia. She showed
each one a tooth lying in a little box—the tooth knocked
out of her mouth by Police Inspector Karabash during his
"questioning." The guests examined the tooth with the
closest attention, as if they had never seen a tooth before.
And with one voice they called Karabash a sonofabitch.

I was sitting not far away from Top Hat. How skinny
he was, how dead white his face looked! His beard, which
had grown out while he was in jail, had changed him. And
Celia had lost her looks too, the way a person does after a
serious illness.

I tried to tell Top Hat that I had doubted his honesty.
But he didn't let me finish. He gave me a little slap on the
back of the head and picked up a piece of halvah from the
table. He put it in front of me on the newspaper which
was being used as a tablecloth.

"You know you love halvah," he said.

His friendly gesture made me feel better. I realized that
he had forgiven me for being such an idiot. But I couldn't
forgive myself for acting the way I did. The business with
Top Hat taught me a hard lesson. It made me understand

that there are unscrupulous people in the world who try to smear and blacken the good name of other people, defenseless people, to gain some advantage for themselves —and that such accusations are not to be believed.

Without even touching the halvah (and I really did love halvah) I got up from the table and dragged my feet homeward. My mother, in a happier mood, was waiting supper for me. As usual, she didn't have much to say.

# 26

## Changes, Big and Small

That summer I saw some of my old school friends again. I was struck by the change in almost every one. The Babenchikov brothers had left the gymnasium and were transformed into pimply-faced soldiers, who at that time were called "voluntary enlisted men." Sasha Bugai had grown much broader in the shoulders. He had matured a lot, fitted himself out with a seaman's cap and begun smoking a pipe. He could even spit like a real sailor.

Munya Blokhin, who was as skinny and fast on his feet as ever, suddenly began to fancy himself a great actor. He dressed (in spite of the heat) in a wide black cotton smock with a tremendous purple scarf tied in a bow, and took to exhausting his admirers by reciting in a tragic voice:

> *I was ready of late to renounce every gladness,*
> *With scorn I looked down on those sated and*
> *proud . . .*

Moreover, he rolled his "r's" so far back in his throat that it sounded like he was gargling.

> *I was gheady of late to ghenounce evghy glad-*
> *ness,*
> *With scoghn I looked down on those sated and*
> *pghoud . . .*

Valka Tuntin now looked just like a fat hog, and Rita Vadzinskaya evidently liked this a lot. I used to meet them together wherever I went. You could see by her face that he was no "creep" to her. But since I was really cured of my old crush on that empty-headed girl, I no longer found her beautiful.

Loboda and Bondarchuk, the brightest students in our class, read Darwin during vacation. They came to the conclusion that there is no God and that religion is a fraud. Grishka Zuyev, with whom they tried to debate the question of the existence of God, refuted all their conclusions with one unanswerable argument; he went straight to Father Melety in Pokrovskaya Church, and denounced them for blasphemy. Father Melety praised the informer, summoned the unbelievers and threatened them with police action.

No less than the others, I had changed too. A fluff of hair suddenly appeared on my upper lip. I dug up a knobbed walking stick somewhere (the same kind that Finti-Monti used to go around with) and I let my hair grow down to my shoulders.

There was a long—a very long—period when my relationship with Marusya didn't improve, for some reason. Even though I secretly admired her, I treated her like a boor, and stubbornly resisted her efforts to enrich my mind with her valuable knowledge.

Once, at dinner time, I said that a certain drawing in the magazine *Niva* was "irrevelant." Marusya frowned and said in her teaching tone of voice that you were supposed to say "irrelevant" and not "irrevelant." But the demon of contradiction was so strong inside me that for a long time after that I still kept right on saying "irrevelant." And this would cause Marusya every single time to repeat:

"Not 'irrevelant' but 'irrelevant.' "

"That's just exactly what I said: 'irrevelant.' "

Instead of the word "spaghetti" I would say "pisghetti" for the sheer pleasure of hearing Marusya correct me over and over:

"Not 'pisghetti' but 'spaghetti.' "

"That's just what I said: 'pisghetti.' "

This used to drive her crazy, but she would try to hold on to her temper and keep repeating with outward calmness:

"No, not 'pisghetti' but 'spaghetti.' "

I thwarted her at every step.

One time she got the idea of taking me for a walk in Alexandrovsky Park, where a deafening military brass band used to play on holidays. Its brass howls carried to the farthest corners of the park. The paths were sprinkled with gravel which crunched unpleasantly under my feet, and there were signs everywhere:

WALKING ON THE GRASS IS STRICTLY FORBIDDEN!

SPOILING THE LAWN IS STRICTLY FORBIDDEN!

## Changes, Big and Small

and so forth and so on.

Marusya herself was getting sick of these strolls in a boring line of other strollers. But she believed that by walking together with me to the accompaniment of music, and getting me used to "cultural relaxation" at the same time, she was sacrificing herself for my sake.

Here too I proved undeserving of her concern. When we were going home after the third or fourth such walk, I announced that I had had it up to here with that park and that I wasn't Madam Shershenevich's lapdog for her to walk around on a leash.

That was crude and unfair. What was the point of wounding someone who thought she was acting for my own good? But just the same I didn't apologize but left Marusya standing there alone, and ran to my Wigwam as fast as my legs would carry me.

But as soon as I became a "young man" and Marusya finished school, our whole life changed in one year. We began making our living by giving lessons. We drummed arithmetic, geography, algebra and Russian grammar into the heads of failing students who were receiving grades of 1 and 2. I outgrew my boyish roughness with the years like measles or scarlet fever. Once Marusya and I were on the road to growing up, we became friends. Our mutual work brought us together. From morning to night we gave lessons to every imaginable variety of blockhead, helping them scramble out of the swamp of 2's they were wallowing in.

Marusya, a natural teacher, showed such untiring perseverance that all the mamas regarded her as a wizard. She could make top-grade students out of dumbbells inside of three or four months.

I tried to imitate her in everything—never to smile during the lesson period, to be just as serious and important-looking as she was. But things never worked out that way with me. By the second or third lesson, I would already be involved in long conversations with my pupils on "irrevelant" subjects: how to catch a tarantula, how to make a reed arrow, how to play pirates and brigands. Not to mention the adventures of Sherlock Holmes, King Solomon's mines and the feats of the bike racer Utochkin.

Marusya scolded me for letting my boys—who were half my age—get too familiar with me. But no matter how I tried to puff myself up, I could never manage to acquire her air of authority. And my long hair didn't help any, either—nor my thick knobbed walking stick, which I tapped impressively on the sidewalk exactly the way Finti-Monti used to do.

Finally, Marusya made her peace with my irresponsibility, as she did with all my other sins; and the friction between us quieted down of its own accord. And that was one more sign that we were both growing up.

Our earnings grew to the point where my mother was finally able to turn down heavy manual labor and could settle down to the work she loved most—embroidering Ukrainian hand towels and shirts. She had been a master of this craft since childhood. She knew every stitch imaginable, from satin stitch to cross-stitch, and she never copied ready-made patterns, but invented her own combinations of designs and colors. At first she gave all her handwork to Subbotsky, who paid her in kopecks and swindled her outrageously. But by the end of the year she had so many customers that Subbotsky's services were no longer required.

My mother worked with love, and people went into raptures over the quality of her needlework. The most excited of all were Mademoiselle Francesca Ricquet and her sister Mademoiselle Malvina, with whom my mother had recently become friendly because of the embroidery.

"A real work of art!" Mademoiselle Francesca would say when Mama showed her some new piece of work. "It belongs not here but in a museum of handicrafts."

Mademoiselle Malvina wouldn't say anything at all, but as a sign of agreement with her sister Francesca she would nod her gray head, on which a bald pink spot was already showing.

And on Great Arnautskaya Street in the house where Top Hat lived, two very important events occurred at about the same time. Celia had a baby boy, Danya, with a head of hair as flaming red as her own. And Malanka, who lived in the cellar, gave birth to twin girls. By mistake, the deacon gave them both the same name, Malanka, when he registered them in the church record books at their christening. Since Malanka's mother, who was a maid in one of the apartments in our house, was also named Malanka, this mistake upset the two older Malankas very much. They didn't calm down until they took my mother's advice and began calling one of the little new Malankas "Natalka" and the other one "Frosya."

Soon after the birth of her children, Malanka left her no-account husband Savelly. She took Natalka and Frosya with her and moved in with Motya, the draymen's cook.

And Malanka started going to people's houses to do day's work. In one place she would do the laundry, in another she washed the windows, in still another she'd take care of other people's children. Once she was liberated from her cellar she instantly changed back into the old Malanka— chipper, tireless, full of energy, mocking, or as we used to say, "a long tongue." Whatever she did, she did with such zest that it made you feel good to watch her. The childless Motya loved Malanka's twins like her own and fed them to bursting out of the common pot.

Themistocles Drakondidi didn't stay behind bars for very long. Soon he was out of jail and back at his old career. His luxuriant beard could be seen once more, waving over his red, blue and green syrups. It was clear that when he divided up the loot with the police, he was generous with them.

From the day when Finti-Monti dragged his shabby, flattened-out suitcase from under the bed, took a forbidden book out of it and solemnly handed it to me, my boyhood came to an end once and for all, irretrievably. And that means the end of my story. For my story is about boyhood.

But just the same I would like to say a few more words before telling you goodbye. First of all about the promise I gave my mother. I kept my word in the end. But not right away, not until much, much later. Timosha and Munya and Ludwig Meier had all been university students for a long time, while I was still considered the same half-baked kid who had been thrown out of the fifth-year class.

The commission which re-examined me in the gymnasium curriculum flunked me twice. Flunked me deliberately, for the same reason that Six-Eyes and Proshka took away my silver crest.

Not until the third year of trying, when I took my exams at the Richelieu Gymnasium where Finti-Monti had recently begun to teach, did I finally receive my graduation certificate without any further obstacles and with very decent marks. It even seemed a bit insulting that the affair which had caused me so much suffering should finish so simply.

I bought myself a university student's cap at the flea market—a used one, so as to look like an old student. This cap had a magic effect on my mother. She, who never liked going out and had almost no acquaintances, suddenly developed an enthusiasm for taking walks with me down the most crowded streets in town. At every opportunity she would get into conversations with whoever came along, just so as to be able to drop the casual remark, "I'd like you to meet my son the university student."

As if set free after a long imprisonment, she became talkative, sociable and curious about the world around her. Dark-browed, stately, with a noble profile and proud carriage, she seemed to have just become aware of her own beauty. For the first time in many years she bought herself a new hat and ordered a winter "rotunda" from the seamstress—a stylish coat without sleeves. And she even went to the theater with Marusya and me to see the celebrated Figner Company when they made a guest appearance.

But she didn't take pride in her son the student for long. Soon a more important sentence crept into her conversation. "My son, you know, is a writer."

And it was true.

The thing I had never dared dream of, the thing that seemed to me the highest possible human happiness, happened to me quite unexpectedly. The local newspaper published a rather long (and not very good) article of mine. That marked the beginning of my literary career, which went on without interruption for sixty-odd years.

I know now from long experience that being a writer, even the most modest and unremarkable writer, is truly a great (though sometimes very difficult) happiness. Even this account of my boyhood was so absorbing for me to write! For as soon as I sat down at my desk and picked up my pen and a piece of blank paper, my childhood returned to me. I was transformed from an old man into a boy; and I was jumping around again like a wild Indian on the clanging iron plate that covered our garbage pit. Once more I was scraping a scorching hot roof with a long spatula. I was sitting on a high notched fence under a ninety-five-degree sun and yelling at the top of my voice, "U-u-tochkin!"

And I will be happier still if you come to share my love for my proud, fearless mother, and for Marusya, Timosha, Finti-Monti, Top Hat, Uncle Foma and Iglitsky. And— shall I admit it? I hope you will also share my hatred for Proshka, Six-Eyes, Zuzya Kozelsky, Zhorka Drakondidi, Savelly and Tuntin and all the rest of the scum who have not yet disappeared completely from our way of life, not finally, not everywhere. They still try to spoil life for the rest of us, *whatever disguise they may wear.* But I would like to think it is easier to deal with them today than it was then, so long ago, in the days I've been trying to tell you about in this book.